From Innocence to Entitlement

A Love and Logic Cure for the Tragedy of Entitlement

Jim Fay

and

Dawn L. Billings, M.A., LPC

2207 Jackson St, Golden, CO 80401-2300

800-338-4065

www.loveandlogic.com

Library of Congress Cataloging-in-Publication Data

Fay, Jim.

From innocence to entitlement : a love and logic cure for the tragedy of entitlement / Jim Fay and Dawn L. Billings.

p. cm.

Includes bibliographical references and index.

1. Egoism in children. 2. Child rearing. I. Billings, Dawn L. II. Title.

BF723.E37F39 2005

649'.7--dc22

2004027986

Project Coordinator: Carol Thomas

Editing by Jason Cook, Denver, CO

Indexing by Douglas J. Easton, New West Indexing, Westminster, CO

Cover design and interior design by

Michael Snell, Shade of the Cottonwood, Topeka, KS

Published and printed in the United States of America.

Contents

Life is always at some turning point.
The important question is, "Who
is responsible for the direction of
the turn?"

—Dawn Billings

Preface

The Evolution of Entitlement

Most of us think of evolution as directional. It is a story about how animals evolve into humans. It sounds logical, even though there are some definite holes in the theory. Nevertheless, many have accepted it without a great deal of resistance. The existence of this theory, and our acceptance of it, have a dramatic impact on how many of us view life on our planet, and evolution appears to be something over which we have no control. This theory of evolution has a great deal in common with the theory of entitlement, except that the theory of entitlement works in reverse. It is a theory of how people are evolving into what resembles a much lower form of humankind, one that is neither humane nor kind. As entitlement evolves in our culture, it threatens to extinguish genuine happiness and success, but we can do something to stop it. Let's look at a quick snapshot of how entitlement has impacted our hearts, our relationships, and our communities.

We build larger malls while downsizing our concern for others. We obsess about how tall the buildings to replace the Twin Towers should be while giving little thought to relationships being destroyed by short tempers. We protect pornographers' right to distribute their so-called art and make billions of dollars in the process, while eliminating school art programs for our children because there are no funds. We have loosened our morals but restricted our kindnesses. Our food is fast and our apologies are slow. We are late to conferences with our children's teachers, but give up early when helping them with their homework. Our remotes are turned on while our ears are turned off.

Global warming is on the rise while love goes cold in half of all marriages. Our politicians stand divided while our national debt multiplies. We fight to clean up the air on our planet but surrender to the pollution of sadistic and degrading lyrics in our music. Parents cannot lay hands on their children but complete strangers are allowed to assault their souls. Courts protect the rights of virtual child pornographers while children are told the pledge of allegiance is unconstitutional. These are the times of low carbohydrates and high cholesterol, baggy clothes and tight fists. Our bodies grow taller while our character is stunted.

It is time to evaluate what we as human beings are evolving into. Entitlement and its cancerous tentacles have infected every area of our lives. What can we do to fight its deadly spread? The cure for the wrath of entitlement is simple. The answer lies in filling our minds with simple but effective strategies of logic, and filling our judgmental and controlling hearts with love.

Introduction

A Note from Jim Fay

We have friends and relatives who devote their lives to protecting their children from inconvenience, disappointment, discomfort, struggle, embarrassment, and any form of delayed gratification. They sacrifice their own well-being and even their financial security to provide for the wants of their children. I'm sure you can cite instances of parents who have driven themselves into bankruptcy in their continuing efforts to protect their grown children from bad financial and personal decisions.

My question to you is: Have you ever seen this work out in a positive way in the long term? How often do the offspring of these parents wake up to recognize that they, themselves, have become spoiled, self-centered, and in need of changing their ways? Have you ever heard of an intensely protected and coddled youngster growing into adulthood and coming to his or her parents to say:

> I owe you so much. You have been overly good to me, and instead of recognizing your love, I developed a severe sense that you owed me everything I got. As a result, I developed a belief that the world owed me happiness and security. This belief has caused me to be chronically unhappy because the more I got, the more I believed that I deserved. I never learned appreciation or humility.

> But here's the good news. I have changed my ways. From now on I will be willing to struggle and earn what I get. I will no longer expect others to provide for me or for my happiness. And better than that, I now have a job and will be setting aside a portion of my salary each month to create an account to provide for you when you can no longer provide for yourself. Thank you, Mom and Dad. I love you and want to be able to take care of you as well as you took care of me during my years of living the life of the entitled.

I have now worked with children, parents, and teachers for over fifty years. Never during my career have I seen this happen. Granted, some strong individuals, with the help of long-term therapy, have come close to achieving this. However, my experience and research tell me that this is no more than a fantasy of parents who overindulge their children.

When I read Dawn Billing's great book *Entitled to Fail, Endowed to Succeed,* I realized that she was eloquently describing the results of overindulging children—the ultimate end being a future of chronic unhappiness built upon a foundation of entitlement beliefs. Dawn clearly points out how an increasing number of Americans look to others as the source of their problems. The "victim mentality" is growing by leaps and bounds in our country and threatens our way of life, as well as the personal achievements and happiness of our citizens.

As I read her book I was taken by the fact that she and I have been working for the same goal, that of helping children grow up to be responsible adults of high character. *Parenting with Love and Logic* is the tool that my partner, Dr. Foster W. Cline, M.D., and I have perfected to assist parents with this formidable task. Over the past thirty years thousands of parents have relied on our parenting techniques. We are rewarded daily as we meet adults who tell us that they were raised with Love and Logic.

Dawn struck up a friendship with me born out of our mutual passions, to help me understand entitlement and to prevent its spread. Now we come together in this book to blend our own unique perspectives and solutions to this problem. Dawn provides the description of entitlement and the devastation it creates. And I provide the techniques for preventing and curing the problem.

It is our hope that this book is clear, practical, and life-changing. For many of you it will give voice to what you already believe, as well as encourage you to continue what you are doing in the face of much of the misinformation and confusion running rampant in our society.

Enjoy!

Jim Fay
President and Founder
Love and Logic Institute, Inc.

The real voyage of discovery consists not in making new landscapes but in having new eyes.

—Marcel Proust

1

Through the Lenses of the Enemy

To complain that life has no joys while there is a single creature who we can relieve by our bounty, assist by our counsels or enliven by our presence, is to lament the loss of that which we possess, and is just as rational as to die of thirst with a cup of water in our hands.

—William Melmoth

• • 1 • •
Through the Lenses of the Enemy

It's not what you look at that matters,
it's what you see.

—Henry David Thoreau

When a five-year-old child enters a room where guests are conversing and announces, "You have had too much adult talk, I want you to stop and be with me right now," that is entitlement.

When a fifteen-year-old girl says, "Why should I vacuum your room, it's not my room," that is entitlement.

When a mother has to abruptly end her phone conversation with her friend because her four-year-old son insists, "You've been on the phone long enough, you talk too much, stop and play with me right now," that is entitlement.

When a child opens a gift and refuses to say thank you and, when challenged, responds, "But it's not what I wanted," that is entitlement.

When a child is asked to apologize for hitting his brother and he refuses, saying, "I don't want to because I hate him," that is entitlement.

When a thirteen-year-old girl screams at her mother, "I hate you, I wish I had never been born into this family," that is entitlement.

When a girl with a closet full of clothes cries, "I have nothing to wear," that is entitlement.

> When a child says, "But that's your job, you're the ones who wanted to be parents," that is entitlement.
>
> When a child says, "I don't have to listen to my teachers, they are idiots," that is entitlement.
>
> When a child says, "I don't want to do chores, no one else has to do chores at their house," that is entitlement.
>
> When a child says, "I have rights and you can't make me," that is entitlement.
>
> When a child says, "I don't want to eat what you're eating, I don't like it, make me something else," that is entitlement.

Entitlement flourishes in the disrespectful demands we hear too often from too many children, including our own. It is fed by the media and nourished by the overindulgence that many parents perpetrate on their children in the name of love. That is how entitlement creeps undetected into our homes, our communities, our schools, and our country. It disguises itself as love and generosity, when all the while it is a thief, out to steal all that is truly valuable in our lives and the lives of our children. As the cancer of entitlement grows ever stronger in our culture, it threatens to extinguish what we want most for our children—genuine happiness and success—while it simultaneously succeeds at tearing our families apart. Entitlement is clever, disguising itself as a friend pretending to bring more to our lives—always more. But entitlement is no friend of humanity, business, or families. It is a lie that exists for only one purpose—to steal our happiness, our respect, our appreciation, and our joy. Entitlement is one of the major reasons why over half of the marriages in this country end in divorce, and why at least a fifth of intact marriages are filled with unhappiness. Entitlement is the reason our schools are in shambles, our families are falling apart, and our children are less motivated to succeed than they have ever been. It is the reason why suicide among school-age kids continues to increase at dramatic and alarming rates. And only we can do something to stop it.

The purpose of this book is to examine how entitlement steals our success, our happiness, and our dreams, while living lives filled with Love and Logic serves to protect us against the wrath of entitlement and actually adds success and happiness back into the equation.

Life for most people is discovered through relationships—our relationship with ourselves, our relationships with others, our community, our country, our planet. It is defined by our ability to relate and be related to in compassionate and positive ways. Entitlement destroys relationships, from intimate to global, by twisting our perceptions toward self-consumption and numbing our feelings of appreciation. Throughout this book, we will examine the many ways entitlement leads us toward failure.

Once we have chosen to create happiness and success in our lives in great abundance, our first step is to learn how to recognize entitlement and its voice. The clearest, simplest way to do this is by learning how to monitor our thoughts. The connection between our thoughts and our lives is inseparable. As Nobel Prize–winning physicist Neils Bohr put it: "What we experience is not external reality, but our interaction with it." In this context, perceptions are profoundly influenced by our beliefs and the thoughts that sustain them. Therefore, you will find entitlement alive and well in all the places where your life simply doesn't work, the places where your relationships are falling apart—areas where you are frustrated, angry, unfulfilled, and dissatisfied. With the examples in this book we will expose the weed of all unhappiness at its root, explain how this weed inspires all failure, and teach you how to pull this destructive weed of despair and misery from your life with simple strategies filled with Love and Logic.

Why should we be concerned about this modern evolution of entitlement and what does it have to do with Love and Logic? Simply put, entitlement destroys what is most important to most of us—happiness and success—while strategies and techniques filled with Love and Logic actually bring both of these qualities more abundantly into our lives.

Ninety-eight percent of over five hundred parents I (Dawn) interviewed at a parenting seminar said that happiness was the thing they wanted most for their children, yet study after study finds our children more depressed and unhappy than ever before. So what is the problem? It is clear that we not only do not understand how to attain and maintain happiness, but also do not understand how it can easily be destroyed.

This book teaches the simple but profound rules of living a life filled with Love and Logic, and why those rules are vital to attaining and maintaining happiness and success in our lives and the lives of our children. But more important, it will teach you to identify the destroyer of happiness and success: *entitlement.* It unveils the destroyer, while arming you and those you love with the knowledge of how to defend against entitlement's destructive wrath.

According to Dr. Henry Grayson, in his book *Mindful Loving,* "Every thought we think, every belief we hold, every interpretation we make of what we perceive, leads to every emotion and action we take."[1] Acting as an enemy of happiness, an *entitled* perspective justifies and even rationalizes dissatisfaction. Entitlement places a stamp labeled Not Enough over the lenses through which we view life. When we feel that we are not getting what we want or deserve, it is easy to justify feeling miserable and dissatisfied.

> Henry Ward Beecher once said, "A proud man is seldom a grateful man for he never thinks he gets as much as he deserves." How often do we, or our children, stop to realize and appreciate the many gifts placed in our laps? We mistakenly believe, in an *entitled* fashion, that whatever good fortune we experience is somehow due us: it is payment just for living. We stand and brush the blessings from our laps as if they were simply crumbs from a meal we refuse to enjoy. We continuously ask for more, and yet this kind of entitled attitude never brings anyone happiness.

How is entitlement able to steal all that is precious in our lives? It simply blinds us to all we have that is valuable. Our world becomes restricted,

1. Henry Grayson, *Mindful Loving,* Penguin Group (USA), 2003.

distorted, and self-absorbed when we view it through the lenses of an entitled perspective, which tell us that whatever we have in our lives is Not Enough. This distorted view creates a breeding ground for selfishness and greed. It perpetuates misery and clouds our vision so that we lose sight of our good fortune, and instead focus on what we believe we lack. Notice that the important word in this sentence is *believe.* If entitlement can succeed at convincing us that ***there is not enough*** or that ***we are not getting what we deserve,*** it can twist our view of the world until it begins to hurt everyone. As entitlement continues to succeed at filtering out abundant data while leaving scarcity and lack in bright focus, seeing scarcity and lack becomes a habit. It becomes automatic, and scarcity and lack begin to occur to us as the truth. This automatic entitled view makes us miserable. Therefore it is easy to understand how an entitled perspective can poison motivation, desire, appreciation, compassion, generosity, reverence, and respect, just to name a few. Most of all, it destroys any opportunity for genuine happiness. Entitled people are unhappy, dissatisfied, ungrateful people.

> *Gratitude unlocks the fullness of life. It turns what we have into enough, and more. It turns denial into acceptance, chaos to order, confusion to clarity. It can turn a meal into a feast, a house into a home, a stranger into a friend. Gratitude makes sense of our past, brings peace for today, and creates a vision for tomorrow.*
>
> —Melody Beattie

So how do we battle the wrath of entitlement as it spreads through our country like a contagious infection? One of the most powerful ways is to use strategies filled with Love and Logic. In my (Dawn's) book *Entitled to Fail, Endowed to Succeed: America's Journey Back to Greatness,* I explain how I believe entitlement gained its hold on our society:

> There is much confusion in this country about entitlement. I believe it stems from our misunderstanding of the pure intent of our founding documents. Many believe that the Declaration of Independence *entitles* all citizens to life, liberty, and the pursuit of happiness. Let's begin by examining what the Declaration of Independence actually states:
>
> > *We hold these truths to be self-evident,*
> > *that all men are created equal,*
> > *that they are endowed by their Creator*
> > *with certain inalienable rights,*
> > *that among these are life, liberty*
> > *and the pursuit of happiness.*
>
> Notice that the word *ENTITLED* does not appear, nor is it implied. Instead this revered statement tells us that we are *ENDOWED* by our Creator with certain inalienable rights. *Endowed* means "to provide with some talent, quality, etc." So let's look at these important sentences once again.
>
> We hold these things to be true, that all men and women are created equal, they are generously provided by their Creator with qualities and talents that cannot be legally or justly taken away or transferred to another. It is their right as citizens to develop and use these talents and qualities of life in the pursuit of liberty and happiness. Clearly our forefathers thought of these rights as gifts and that we should recognize their value and choose to be responsible for developing and using them.
>
> The word *entitled,* on the other hand, means: "to be given a *right*

to demand or receive."[2] Endowed connotes *gift*, where as entitled connotes *right to demand*. Within this powerful distinction we discover the difference between happiness, fulfillment, meaning and purpose; and misery, selfishness, greed, and lack. Entitlement causes us to believe that we have a *right to demand*. We begin to believe that the world we live in owes us something, but the payment is never enough.

When my (Dawn's) youngest son was five years old, he collected Teenage Mutant Ninja Turtles. There were a great number of them and after a while he had accumulated approximately sixty. Sixty plastic turtles is a large number of action figures, so you can imagine my surprise when he came to me one morning with a picture showing all the turtles. He complained about the fact that there were *three* that he did not have. He wasn't making himself happy with the fact that he was very fortunate and blessed to have so many. He was making himself miserable because of his perceived lack.

Perceived lack is one of entitlement's favorite weapons. Another of entitlement's favorite weapons is the thought It's Not Fair. It is especially dangerous when we put them both together and we experience the belief that "it's not fair that I don't have all that I should have."

I explained to my son that I would not consider purchasing another turtle for him until he showed proper gratitude for the ones he owned. I asked him to tell me the names of all the turtles he owned and why he liked them. When he was through with this exercise he was not only tired, but also aware once more of how many turtles he had. He said, "I didn't know how many I had until I had to remember them." His Not Enough perspective changed dramatically with the opportunity to

2. *Webster's New Universal Unabridged Dictionary.*

count his turtles. He suddenly *remembered,* or in reality, reminded himself of, how fortunate he was. So many times happiness comes from reminding ourselves of what we already possess simply by taking inventory.

> *Gratitude is born in hearts that take time to count up past mercies.*
>
> —CHARLES E. JEFFERSON

As the turtle story illustrates, the lenses of *endowment* are colored with words like Blessed, Fortunate, and Lucky. A *perspective of endowment* invites us to take inventory of all that is good in our lives. When we feel abundant, we behave in kind, respectful, and generous ways. This view of the world creates a vastly different internal experience than that created through lenses colored with Not Enough and Life's Unfair. Love and Logic strategies aid us not only in remembering our good fortune, but also in assuming the personal responsibility necessary in order to feel confident, competent, and abundant in life.

> *Yes, there is a "secret to happiness"—and it is gratitude. All happy people are grateful, and ungrateful people cannot be happy. We tend to think that it is being unhappy that leads people to complain, but it is truer to say that it is complaining that leads to people becoming unhappy.*
>
> —DENNIS PRAGER

A perfect example of an attitude of endowment is beautifully expressed in the words of George Bernard Shaw:

> This is the true joy in life—that being used for a purpose recognized by yourself as a mighty one. That being a force of nature, instead of a feverish, selfish little clod of ailments and grievances complaining that the world will not devote itself to making you happy. I am of the opinion that my life belongs to the whole community and as long as I live it is my privilege to do for it whatever I can. I want to be thoroughly used up when I die, for the harder I work the more I live. I rejoice in life for its own sake. Life is no brief candle to me. It's a sort of splendid torch which I've got to hold up for the moment and I want to make it burn as brightly as possible before handing it on to future generations.

The above quote is void of entitlement's dark self-highlighting colors. Instead it is rich with power, action, and optimism. Shaw's words are born out of an attitude of endowment. Entitlement, with its lenses of Not Enough, Life's Not Fair, and I Deserve, asks, "What's in it for me?" or insists, "I am entitled. Give it to me!" In contrast, endowment, with its lenses of I Am Blessed and I Am Fortunate, asks, "In what way can my gifts and talents be used to benefit the world, as well as myself?" It states, "I rejoice in life for its own sake, and as long as I live, it is my privilege to do for others whatever I can."

2

Entitlement Thrives on Disrespect

We do not love people so much for the good they have done us, as for the good we have done them.

—Leo Tolstoy

2
Entitlement Thrives on Disrespect

Life was a lot simpler when what we honored was father and mother rather than all major credit cards.

—Robert Orben

Entitlement's incursions are felt in all aspects of our lives, but like a mosquito in stagnant water, it thrives best in a pool of disrespect. Once we stop extending basic courtesies to each other, our problems multiply quickly. Some people believe that the gift of free speech gives them the right to inflict their deficit of decency and lack of consideration on each other—because legally, it does. But when we choose to treat another human being with disrespect we are really only cheating ourselves and those we love out of a great and wonderful connection. In Dawn's book *Entitled to Fail, Endowed to Succeed: America's Journey Back to Greatness*, she explains:

> Some people believe that free speech requires no self-discipline. They believe it not only gives them a license to speak their opinions, but to be rude in the process. Hatefully, they will speak without restraint in ways that are at best the antitheses of consideration. If you happen to glance at them, aghast at their treatment of another human being, they might glare back at you and curtly retort, "What's your problem? It's a free country. I can say anything I want, any time I want." I doubt, however, that these same zealous patriots of the first amendment would have deep and abiding appreciation for someone who chose to treat them similarly. Their reaction to equal treatment would be quite different. It would go

something like, "What's wrong with those idiots? Don't they have any manners?"

Manners ... what are they and where do they come from? And more important, why do they matter? Aren't manners some ancient, unnecessary remnant from times long past when our grandparents proudly reveled in our remembrance to wipe our hands on our napkins instead of our sleeves? *Webster's New Universal Unabridged Dictionary* defines manners as "ways of social behavior; deportment, especially with reference to polite conventions." The same dictionary defines deportment as "the manner of conducting or bearing oneself; behavior; demeanor; conduct; management." Why in the world, in the year 2003, in a book about entitlement, would I bring up something as mundane as manners? The answer is simple: Without a shared basic code of decency, conduct, and behavior, it is impossible to benefit from the blessings of family or community. If you have ever been surprised, aghast, ashamed, frightened, or humiliated by the behavior of a complete stranger, or worse, someone you love, you may have wondered if some members of our society might not benefit from a few management skills, lessons in conduct, and more considerate behavior.

Manners are interesting things. They are disarming, charming, but most of all, respectful. They are our first introduction to respect. This introduction is critical because we can only learn to respect ourselves through learning to respect others. Most people want to be respected and yet have not learned to be respectful. Being held in a position of respect can feed an ego, but the humility and grace learned through being respectful feeds a soul.

Respect, like love, needs to be thought of as a verb. In school we learn that verbs are "action words." We must live respect as a verb in our lives and inspire our children, our friends, and our co-workers to do the same. As parents, we have a tendency to imagine that manners should come as standard equipment with our children; but alas, they do not. Manners must be learned. Manners are important in any society because they teach an important form of humility. They shift us away from our narcissistic gaze into the pond. When we say, "Thank You," "Please," "Excuse me," and "You're welcome," for example, we have to stop for a moment to notice what is going on in the world around us. Who is interacting with us, sharing with us, serving us?

Knowledge must come through action.

—SOPHOCLES

In conclusion, manners are the foundation of respect and respect is what Love and Logic techniques are built around. Good old-fashioned manners—thoughtfulness, courtesy, kindness, politeness, consideration, graciousness, and basic etiquette—all culminate in a respectful and appreciative way of relating to the world and the people in it. Showing and sharing our manners causes us to loosen the death grip on our narcissism long enough to realize that there are others in the world, and recognize the contributions they are making on our behalf. It is difficult for many of us to give up our attempts to be the center of the universe; in fact, as parents we often train our children that they are just that—the center of our lives. Love and Logic techniques allow us to balance our relationships, with each person being responsible for his or her choices and the consequences of those choices.

Parenting with Love and Logic relies on three simple laws. We call them the three E's. We must remember that children learn through ***Example*** and ***Experience***, and we support their learning best when we respond with genuine ***Empathy***. When we understand that we teach by example, we realize that it is vital that we live courteous, balanced, grateful, self-responsible lives, and expect our children to do the same. Modeling is one of the most powerful teachers at our disposal. If you want your children to behave in respectful, appreciative, self-responsible ways, first make the necessary commitment to be respectful, appreciative, and self-responsible. Appreciation, respect, and self-responsibility, when given our attention and practice, become habits—excellent habits. Habits become a part of our character, and our character becomes our destiny. People who are mannerly and appreciative are generous. They live and work from a position of abundance. When people feel abundant, they see more possibilities and opportunities in their lives. Therefore they are happier.

> *Our rewards in life will always be in exact proportion to the amount of consideration we show toward others.*
>
> —Earl Nightingale

Manners, respect, consideration, and appreciation are simply habits, just as an attitude of entitlement is a habit. The Love and Logic techniques you will be reviewing in the next chapters will be some of the best habits that you or your children can cultivate. We will be weaving our three E's throughout the pages of this book in order for you to fully understand how to use them and when. Only you can decide which habits serve you, which habits bless you and make your relationships happy and successful. Only you can decide which habits break your relationships and the hearts of those you love. You have a choice. You can develop entitled habits that cause you to believe, "*You owe me. Pay up!*" and by the way, "*That's not enough.*" Or worse, "***You** are not enough.*" Or you can focus on generous habits that move you to say, "*Thank you for the ways in which you serve my life. I notice them and appreciate you.*" You must choose which habits to develop and which habits to break.

> *Excellence is not an act but a habit. The things you do the most are the things you will do the best.*
>
> —Marva Collins

3

Today's Culture for Parents and Children

The content of your thoughts and personal beliefs can be proven by a single indicator—your current results.

—James A. Ray

3

Today's Culture for Parents and Children

Identity requires responsibility, because without responsibility there is no self-respect.

—Charles Handy

William J. Doherty, PhD, tells us in his book *Take Back Your Kids* that there is a new culture for children. Teachers sadly will confirm this. It appears that our children have become *consumers* of parental services. And parents are viewed as providers of parental services and *brokers* of community services for children. We as parents have been led to believe that our *job* as "good" parents is to serve and provide our children with a plethora of activities and rewards, so that they can have every chance at success in today's fast-paced, competitive society. This imbalance of services *provided on demand* comes with a high price tag. It teaches our children that they are to be served, but not how to serve. It causes the concept of benefit or service to become a line that travels in just one direction—toward them! According to Dr. Doherty:

> What gets lost is the other side of the human equation: children bearing responsibilities to their families and communities. In a balanced world, children are expected not only to receive from adults but also to actively contribute to the world around them, to care for the younger and the infirm, to add their own marks to the quality of family life, and to contribute to the common good in their school and communities.[1]

1. William J. Doherty, *Take Back Your Kids*, Sorin Books, 2000.

When parents see themselves *primarily* as providers of services, they end up confused and even anxious. Not that providing services isn't a part of what it means to be a parent, but the key word in that sentence is *part.* If parents see themselves as *only* providers of services, they can end up insecure about whether they are providing *enough.* If they listen to messages from other confused parents, the media, and the inflated and entitled demands of their children, they can begin to feel that no matter how much they do and give, it is *never enough.* That is exactly how entitlement slyly infects our families. It makes sense that in a competitive, capitalistic economy, the service provider must at all costs avoid disappointing the customer. The service provider must strive to offer the newest and best, but when this thinking is applied to the family, it is a recipe for disaster that creates insecure parents and unhappy, entitled kids.

Most parents wouldn't think twice about setting limits for their children in situations where danger is clearly present. For example, not one parent would hesitate to stop a child from playing in the middle of a busy intersection. The confusion arises when parents are not sure of what is harmful and what is helpful. There is higher education for everything except the two areas where we need it most—parenting and relationships. Therefore many parents don't understand that what they think is love and service actually harms their children. Dr. Doherty believes:

> When parents serve their children too much, they identify too closely with their successes and failures. It becomes hard to tell whether the child's athletic events are more for the child or the parents. Lower academic grades produce parental outrage against the teacher. Parents cannot deny a request for the latest designer clothing item, because having one's teenager be "out of it" with peers is as unacceptable to the parent as it is to the young person. In serving too much and expecting too little, we end up confusing our children's needs with our own. Their insecurities become ours, and our insecurities become theirs.[2]

2. William J. Doherty, *Take Back Your Kids,* Sorin Books, 2000.

We must remember that children get their entitled attitudes from the same culture that feeds self-centered adults. This is the "ME" generation. We live more isolated from community than ever before. Most people do not know their neighbors' names, let alone do they offer to be of service to them. In fact, service for most children is a one-way paved road that leads straight to themselves. Our children begin to believe that all roads lead to Rome and that they *are* Rome. I (Dawn) cannot think of service and contribution without remembering an incident that changed forever the life of my oldest son, Tony. I will allow him to tell it in his own words:

> It was my junior year in high school. My grades were up, my social life was thriving, and everything seemed to be running smoothly. My mom had this thing about "contribution." She kept telling me that people are only truly great when they benefit the lives of others. Benefit had always been a line in my direction, and from where I stood, that was just fine. But Mom was relentless. She was obsessed with this "giving something back" thing.
>
> It was a Thursday, and I was bored. I hated my first period AP US History, but not today. I had signed up earlier in the week to donate to a blood bank that was visiting school. This was awesome. I would be able to skip AP US History, not to mention get my mom off my back about this "contribution" thing. I thought *this must be my day.*
>
> The donation process was simple; wait in line with your friends, talk with people, sit down in a chair for 10 minutes, and donate a pint of blood. How hard can that be? However, I had not accounted for the needles, the sight of blood, and pain. I almost fainted when I saw the needle, not to mention what I felt when they stuck it in my arm. I thought that this was going to be people eating cookies and drinking orange juice. I guess I was wrong; this was *definitely* not my day. I was weak, and in pain. I felt shaky, and the large hole in the middle of my left arm leaking blood from my vein wasn't pleasing me. My third period Economics teacher told me I looked white as a ghost, and to go to the nurse and lie down and rest. *"My mom had better really give me credit for this. I am glad this is over,*

and I never have to do this again," I thought as I was making my way to the nurse's office. *"I should've stayed in AP US History."*

The following Saturday morning the phone rang. I let it ring until someone else finally answered it. Saturday mornings meant sleeping in, not answering phones. There was a brief pause after the phone rang, then suddenly my mom burst through my door and shoved the phone in my face. She insisted that I wake up and take the call. All I was told was that the Red Cross was on the phone. *"Red Cross? Didn't they have better things to do than to harass me on a Saturday morning?"* I took the phone and spoke to a woman on the other end about my donated blood. My mom only heard one side of the conversation, which went something like this.

"Yes, this is Tony Billings."

"Yes, on Thursday."

"No, I don't remember."

"What?!"

"Are you sure? Have you checked it twice?"

"This can't be happening to me. Why me?"

"Yes, yes. I understand."

"Yes I will come down to the Red Cross immediately on Monday morning."

"Yes. Okay. I can't believe this."

"Good-bye."

I reached over to hang up the phone. I was fully awake now. My mom stood there staring at me. Her color was off, and she wasn't looking too good.

"What's wrong Mom?" I asked as I found the cradle for the phone. "Are you all right?"

"I'm fine. What about you? What did they want with you?" There was stark terror in her eyes. I guess if I was a parent on the other end of the phone call with Red Cross, I might have looked terrified as well.

"You are not going to believe this," I said.

"Try me," she replied without a smile.

"They said that I have the cytomegalovirus."

"What does that mean?" she nervously inquired.

"I have *special baby blood.* I had a virus when I was a newborn and I developed antibodies to it. I also have O negative blood and that makes me a universal donor. This cytomegalovirus kills newborn babies who are unable to build up strong enough immune systems to fend off this virus. Because this blood type (CMV O-) is rare, they issue me a special donors card that I must show every time I donate. They want me to give blood every 90 days too. I *hate* giving blood," I complained.

"Oh my goodness. I can't believe it. You have special baby blood? You are so blessed." She seemed to really be enjoying this.

"That depends on which end of the needle you are on, now doesn't it?" I whined.

In the months ahead I got to see some of the babies who are now carrying a part of me with them to protect them. I couldn't believe the feeling. It wasn't anything like I expected. I have to tell you the circle of giving is much better than a line in one direction could ever be. I guess that is why they say love is a circle.

Mom got her wish. I found a way to contribute and make a difference in the lives of others. It wasn't what I imagined. I guess I thought that I would pick my gift to give to the world, myself. What I have learned is that sometimes God, in his wisdom, picks for us. Mom had always told me that the giving isn't as much about what you give, or whom you give it to, as it is about what it makes of you when you do it. As hard as I had attempted to change the circle of giving into a line pointed in my direction, to my benefit, I did not succeed. Mom was right, my contribution is small compared to what it gives back to me, and I am thankful that God "sticks" with those of us who need a little extra push to share.

Tony's story is a perfect example of how entitlement's one-way line of self-absorption can be turned into the circle of service that it was meant to be. This is an important lesson not simply because it makes a difference in the lives of others, but also because it makes the biggest difference in the life of the one serving.

> *The major value in life is not what you get. The major value in life is what you become. That is why I wish to pay fair price for every value. If I have to pay for it or earn it, that makes something of me. If I get it for free, that makes nothing of me.*
>
> —Jim Rohn

Another powerful culture that has infected parents and their children is the culture of therapeutic parenting.[3] When we think of therapists, most of us picture an environment that is attentive, accepting, nondirective, nonjudgmental, accepting, and self-focused. Many parents have gotten confused and believe that this is the kind of environment that they need to create for their children. The therapeutic culture of parenting suggests that children's psyches are fragile, and easily broken.

This therapeutic culture was born out of three psychological gospels. The gospel of Freud, which tells us that our past experiences dramatically influence our present and future, and that therefore it is important to protect our children from distress and discomfort that might cause a fracture in their fragile egos. Freud also tells us that insight is curative and that in essence, if children were simply listened to and allowed to express their underlying feelings of frustration and anger, their insight into the underlying causes of those feelings could save them later dysfunction.

3. William J. Doherty, *Take Back Your Kids,* Sorin Books, 2000.

Following the gospel of Freud came the gospel of Carl Rogers and the humanist movement. Rogers insisted that all children are innately good. Therefore, all we have to do as caretakers is water that goodness and it will grow. This was the birth of unconditional positive regard and the self-esteem movement. If parents were to work hard to ensure that their children are not put in any distressful situations that might have lingering consequences, and if we were to create an environment where the little marvelous miracles we call children are watered every day with praise and appreciation for their unique talent of being born, we could grow appreciative, thriving, loving, giving, focused people who are contributions to themselves and the world.

Following the gospels of Sigmund Freud and Carl Rogers came the gospel of B. F. Skinner, who reduced behavior to the level of rats, birds, and dogs. He told us that behavior was simply a function of contingent rewards. So we decided that along with ensuring that our children had no distress that could cause later impairments, had the perfect environment full of praise and appreciation, and had the perfect contingent rewards, as parents we could be guaranteed that our children, at the age of eighteen, would be handsome, successful, compassionate, focused, driven, and generous young adults.

The pressure these theories put upon the shoulders of parents and teachers is enormous. Parents and teachers have been taught that, anytime a child chooses to fail, instead of looking at failure as a potential opportunity for the child to learn and grow, they should rush to pick up the slack and find a way to improve the environment, lower the stress, and increase the praise and rewards. The problem is that the philosophies born out of these three theories are fatally flawed. The problem lies in the fact that these three theories support the same major misconception. They tell us that our children's behavior, character, and eventual success are dependent on something other than themselves. This is one of the greatest misconceptions of the twentieth century. Our children's behavior, character, and eventual success has not nearly as much to do with what happens *to them* as it does with what they *choose to become* in spite of, or even because of, what happens to them. This is where our second Love and Logic "E," learning through ***Experience***, is so important.

One of the greatest teachers our children will ever have is the life experience born out of the natural consequences of their choices. But allowing our children to experience the natural consequences of their poor choices is often difficult for parents to tolerate, especially if they have been indoctrinated into the therapeutic parenting culture.

The most dangerous myths of the therapeutic parenting culture are:

1. ***Children are fragile.*** The reality, according to mountains of research, is that children are not nearly as fragile as we have made them out to be. Once they are infected with the entitlement virus, their behaviors can become out of control and extreme, but that does not result from them being fragile; it is a result of them becoming entitled. In fact, most research tells us that if underlying love, care, and attachment are present, most children are extremely resilient in the face of ordinary kinds of mistakes, nonabusive anger, and parents' inevitable episodes of self-centeredness, inattentiveness, and overreaction.[4]

2. ***A child's uniqueness is more valuable than their ability to conform.*** The myth that each child is a one-of-a-kind flower that cannot bloom as beautifully if they are expected to conform to the pattern of the garden not only is incorrect, but also actually detracts from the potential of the child to develop their uniqueness. It takes an ability to conform and an ability to express unique gifts and talents to become the contributing human beings that best serve others.

3. ***Parents do not have direct influence over their children, especially teenagers.*** Therefore parents do not put up the kind of fight necessary to help their children grow. The truth is that children definitely benefit from both love and limits. We cannot allow the societal zeitgeist, marketing of Madison Avenue, television, sports, pop stars, or what's cool at school to raise our children. We must parent. We must set the limits, determine the values that will be revered in our homes, and stand for

4. William J. Doherty, *Take Back Your Kids,* Sorin Books, 2000.

something important so our children will not fall for things too small for their potential. These limits must be created out of a loving concern that can be tangibly felt by our children. If our children believe that the limits we set for them are genuinely born out of our love for them, even when they resist them, they will at a deep level respect them.

4. ***Self-esteem is critical for children to succeed in life and it is our jobs as teachers and parents to provide it.*** Children do not need *self*-esteem as much as they need to learn what it means *to esteem.* They need to develop an intrinsic sense of their value and worth. This occurs when they learn to esteem not only themselves, but also their families, their teachers, their leaders, their friends, and their country. When we have learned to esteem another, we cannot help but develop esteem within ourselves. But when the focus is on *self* instead of *esteem,* our children can become victims of the blinding effects of entitlement to the point that it steals their peace, confidence, worth, and happiness.

4

Entitled to Self-Esteem

You may be good, but what are
you good for?

—Stephen R. Covey

4
Entitled to Self-Esteem

To do the useful thing, to say the courageous thing, to contemplate the beautiful thing: that is enough for one man's life.

—T. S. Eliot

We all decry the social epidemics of our time. Experts warn of the increase in drug abuse, teen pregnancy, and even more terrifying, the recent upsurge in children killing children, as well as the overall rise of violence on our streets and in our schools. The epidemic that we might not have the awareness to decry is the personal and social epidemic that supports and feeds the rest: entitlement.

In the past three decades the United States has seen a three hundred percent increase in adolescent suicide and a thousand percent increase in adolescent depression. Why? Some say our children are suffering from a lack of self-esteem; others argue that the "self-esteem movement" itself is in fact one of the culprits. In this chapter we will dissect and carefully examine this characteristic called "self-esteem" and explore both sides of a national debate around this psychological construct.

Authentic self-esteem deserves more serious research and ongoing dialogue. We need to ask, "What *is* self-esteem?" and "Is the way we are defining self-esteem, understanding it, teaching it, and inspiring its growth in our children working?" We need to find ways to use objective research in developing strategies that aid children in growing into happy, respectful, contributing human beings who can share in the responsibilities and pleasures of living in an emotionally intelligent, compassionate, inclusive society. This national debate about what self-esteem is and isn't, and how we believe it impacts our children's behaviors and choices for their lives, will identify holes in our current self-esteem philosophies where entitlement can take root and grow unhindered. This essential debate is positive because it forces us to carefully dissect this vital attribute and define it more clearly.

Most studies on self-esteem have correlated the social epidemics we refer to at the beginning of this chapter to the breakdown of family and community support systems used to nurture healthy self-esteem. Although perspectives on how to strengthen and supplement these support systems may vary, most parents, educators, counselors, and community leaders believe that developing healthy, authentic self-esteem in our youth is one of our most effective and promising means of preventing destructive behavior. However, the actual psychological construct *self-esteem* begs confusion. *Webster's New Universal Unabridged Dictionary* defines "self-esteem" in two ways:

1. belief in oneself; self-respect
2. undue pride in oneself

As you can see, the definitions are not the same. One creates an environment for success, the other an environment for disillusionment and failure. In the *New York Times Sunday Magazine,* Lauren Slater wrote an article in February 2004 titled "The Trouble with Self-Esteem." Slater claims that the main objective of school self-esteem programs is "to dole out huge heapings of praise, regardless of actual accomplishment." As you can see, Slater is working off of the second definition from *Webster's.* If there is even a small minority of teachers or parents who believe that doling out heaped praise, regardless of any accomplishment, is the way to successfully build their children's self-esteem, it is imperative that we, as advocates for families and children, take the time to evaluate, understand, and dissect current strategies and then clarify what practices best aid children in building an authentic sense of value and self-worth.

Experts and advocates for the "self-esteem movement" believe that it continues to represent the cutting edge in cultivating healthy people and healthy communities. Moreover, they believe it represents our most promising and effective means of building social capital and developing sustainable solutions to our most persistent societal problems. In 1988, assemblyman John Vasconcellos charged the California Task Force to "Promote Self-Esteem and Personal and Social Responsibility," to lead a public study to investigate whether healthy, authentic self-esteem correlates with various troubling behaviors including violence, drug abuse, welfare dependency, and school failure. In its 1990 report, the task force formulated its definition of "self-esteem," based on two years of research, public polling, and expert deliberation, as "our capacity to appreciate our own worth and importance, *to be accountable for ourselves, and to act responsibly toward others.*"[1] As you can see, this definition flows out of the first definition from *Webster's* but adds two vital actions to the dictionary definitions. The *Webster's* definitions are based simply on a feeling or belief held by a person. The task force's definition calls for action—calls for a person *to be personally accountable* and *to act responsibly toward others.* This definition not only better serves our children and our hopes for them, but also succeeds in balancing the first word in this two-word construct: *self.* The definition developed by the task force alters the focus of self-esteem from that of a *feeling* and morphs it into a *foundation.* Self-esteem, when encouraged as simply a feeling, fails children. Feelings are fickle. Self-esteem must be encouraged as a foundation of a child's character, supported by actions and choices that prove the child's value to him- or herself. The only way to develop authentic self-esteem is to earn it. No amount of praise can create it. Only by taking actions that a child believes have value can the seed of self-esteem be nurtured. This seed then grows into character. Exploring how to build self-esteem as a foundation based on actions that build a child's sense of worth is the focus of this chapter.

1. John Vasconcellos, Robert Reasoner, Michele Borba, Len Duhl, and Jack Canfield, "In Defense of Self Esteem," 2004.

At the end of each day, you should play back the tapes of your performance. The results should either applaud you or prod you.

—Jim Rohn

So what do we mean when we say that the only way to develop a real and legitimate sense of self-worth is to earn it? Let us explain. Some parents, in the name of love, attempt to protect their children from any experience that might be emotionally difficult for them, but what is worse, some attempt to protect themselves from the emotional difficulty of watching their children experience legitimate and just consequences. Protecting children from life's inevitable hard work and the natural consequences of poor choices does not enhance their sense of self; in fact, research shows that it drastically diminishes it.

Armies of American teachers and American parents have expended great energy and efforts to protect and honor the feelings of children. They have done this, they believe, in order to protect and bolster their children's self-esteem, and yet the way they have been going about it actually erodes children's sense of worth.

Dr. E. P. Seligman and his associates set out to understand and identify in advance the most vulnerable ten- to twelve-year-old children in order to teach these children a set of cognitive and social skills that would prevent depression. What they discovered was shocking. A generation of feeling-centered self-esteem approaches—the approaches we rely on heavily in our homes and our schools today—had failed the very children they had been designed to serve. According to Dr. Seligman's research findings, emphasizing how a child feels at the expense of what the child does—mastery, persistence, overcoming frustration and boredom and meeting a challenge—parents and teachers are making this generation of children more vulnerable to depression.[2]

Four large-scale studies have proven that the actual esteem of American children, during this era of raising our children to *feel* good about themselves, has never been lower. As Americans have made feeling good and boosting self-esteem in children a primary aim, the incidence of depression has skyrocketed and feelings of self-esteem have actually plummeted. According to Dr. Seligman:

> Our society has changed from an achieving society to a feel-good society. Up until the early 1960's, achievement was the most important goal to instill in our children. This goal was then overtaken by twin goals of happiness and high self-esteem. This fundamental change consists of two trends. One is toward more individual satisfaction and more individual freedom; consumerism, recreational drugs, daycare, psychotherapy, sexual satisfaction, grade inflation. The other is the slide away from individual investment in endeavors larger than the self: God, Nation, Family, Duty. ... [T]he feel-good society, as it overtook the doing-well society, created new opportunities and new freedoms along with new perils. One peril is experiencing difficulty finding meaning in life. ... The individual, the consuming self, isolated from larger entities, is a very poor site for a meaningful life. However, the bloated self is fertile for the growth of depression.[3]

This is what Dr. Seligman and his associates discovered:

- Children need to fail as well as succeed. Failure teaches them many things, but most important, it teaches them how to succeed. People

2. Dr. E. P. Seligman, 2004, available at www.AuthenticHappiness.com.
3. Ibid.

who succeed in life are those who use their failures in deciding how to respond next time. This is called perseverance. Success isn't found in the number of times our children succeed, but in the number of times they are willing to risk failure and what they decide to do after their inevitable failures occur.

> *Failure is only the opportunity*
> *to more intelligently begin again.*
>
> —Henry Ford

- Children need to feel sad and disappointed on occasion (especially when regret and sadness are appropriate reactions to inappropriate choices or behaviors). Not that we would ever purposefully bring sadness to our children; life has a way of taking care of that without any help from us. But we must teach our children that sadness is itself a teacher. Sadness should be respected. Feeling sad, disappointed, or rejected at times is an inevitable part of the human experience. We must encourage children's opportunities to develop the courage and to persevere and withstand sadness, disappointment, and rejection. We should share stories of famous rejections. *Gone with the Wind* was rejected thirty-eight times before it went on to become a classic novel and movie. Dr. Seuss was turned away twelve times before his first book was accepted, and he went on to become one of the most famous children's writers ever to live; now "Islands of Adventure" has a beautiful theme area for children built around his genius, and major motion pictures have been made of his work. *War and Peace* was rejected ten times before going on to become a masterpiece. Jim Henson, the beloved Muppeteer, was rejected for twenty years. Now, even after his death, his genius enriches the lives of children and adults alike. Every month for twenty years, the great poet Gertrude Stein's poems were rejected. Decca Records turned down the sole rights to record the Beatles in 1962, saying, "We don't like their sound; they'll never be popular." They went on to become one of the most famous bands in history. Brittany Spears lost her Star Search battle as a young girl and yet went on to become one of the biggest pop stars of the millennium. When children begin to understand that rejection is often simply a precursor to success, it aids them in becoming more hardy, focused, and persistent individuals—people who approach their opportunities expecting to succeed, and who don't quit when things are difficult.

Success is how high you bounce
after you hit bottom.

—General George S. Patton

- Children need to be occasionally anxious and angry, frustrated and emotionally challenged. It is through these frustrations and emotional challenges that our sense of self is forged. Often, it is in these darker moments of our lives that we discover who we are and the fabric of which we are made.

Far better is it to dare mighty things,
to win glorious triumphs,
even though checkered by failure,
than to take rank with those poor spirits
who neither enjoy much nor suffer much,
because they live in the gray twilight
that knows neither victory nor defeat.

—Theodore Roosevelt

Parents who insist upon shielding their children from disappointments, or the consequences born of bad choices, deprive their children of the opportunity to develop the accountability and responsibility the task force referred to in its definition of "self-esteem." *Parenting with Love and Logic* tells us that when we impulsively rush to protect our children from failure, we deprive them of learning some of their most valuable skills. We deprive them of the opportunity to find creative ways out of their discomfort. If, when they encounter obstacles, we leap to bolster self-esteem, to soften the blows, and to distract them with congratulatory ebullience, we make it harder for them to truly achieve mastery. And if we deprive them of mastery, we weaken self-esteem just as certainly as if we were to belittle, humiliate, and physically thwart them at every turn. By rewarding our children with cheap, undeserved successes, we can, against everything that we desire, create expensive failures.

> *What lies behind us and what lies*
> *in front of us are but tiny matters as*
> *compared to what lies within us.*
>
> —Ralph Waldo Emerson

Our job as a nation, a community, and a family is to aid our children in becoming citizens with great integrity, people whose words have meaning, friends and neighbors whose actions can be trusted, people endowed with esteem. Schools have become breeding grounds of entitlement. We must make safe environments where children can once again learn from their failures. We must not protect our children from the very experiences that have the potential to teach them some of their greatest lessons, for it is these same experiences that aid them in the development of their character and values.

All values must be won by contest and after they have been won, they must be defended.

—Jim Rohn

Children need to fail occasionally. Not just for failure's sake, but for the lessons failure teaches each of us. Therefore we must provide opportunities for children to fail, even change our thinking about failure and begin to get a little excited about it. Our emphasis must shift from having our children achieve perfection to having them pursue greatness.

There are two illustrations that can help us understand the difference between perfection and greatness. Imagine a perfect pristine china figurine. If it falls and hits a hard surface and loses a finger or gets its face chipped, it loses part of its perceived value. Falling, chipping, or breaking is perceived as greatly damaging, such that the value of the statue could be destroyed. This is the perception of perfection. Mistakes, failures, falling short—all are indications of our decreasing value.

Now consider the idea of greatness. We will use Michelangelo's block-of-marble analogy. Michelangelo, when asked how it was possible that he could create such great beauty out of an enormous piece of stone, would reply that he simply chipped away everything that didn't belong. Every chip, every break brought him closer to the greatness within.

We must create an environment where children are encouraged to be artists of their talents, where they are encouraged to take risks, stretch themselves, fall short, get up, and try again. This will greatly aid them in developing their "capacity to appreciate their own worth and importance, *to be accountable for themselves, and to act responsibly toward others.*" We should consider grading students for their efforts toward carving out the greatness within themselves, not just for their parroting of information back to their instructors.

The trouble with most of us is that we would rather be ruined by praise than saved by criticism.

—Norman Vincent Peale

Dr. Seligman tells us that children can benefit from the experience of feeling anxious, emotionally challenged, and frustrated. These feelings of discomfort force them to discover ways of resolving conflict, both internally and externally. We develop some of our greatest strengths out of our distress, especially when we are forced to own our problems. Owning our problems motivates us toward solution and resolution. As we stated before, we are not saying that children need to be placed in situations that can emotionally or physically harm them. We are saying that all children will find themselves in challenging situations naturally as they attempt to navigate their way through the stresses of school, friendships, family conflicts, and life. These are the situations through which they need to be allowed to contemplate and discover themselves. This is where our empathy and guidance provide the love and consideration children need, while our belief in them and their abilities to make good decisions aids them in developing a logical and practical view of how to handle their lives.

Dr. Seligman tells us that children need to feel sad at times, especially if they have behaved inappropriately or hurt someone else. Sadness is an inevitable experience of life and an appropriate consequence for unwise, dangerous, and defiant decisions that result in unpleasant outcomes. These times of sadness and remorse strengthen a child's muscle of conscience, and also allow a child to begin to develop the empathy that he or she will need for implementing their Love and Logic strategies in their present and future relationships. This empathy ultimately leads to compassion for others.

Our children need to experience their mistakes. They need their remorse. They need their opportunities for retribution in order to be encouraged and honored—not simply because it is the emotionally intelligent and mature thing to do, but also because it teaches them how to relate to others in positive, compassionate ways, and helps them earn their rightful place in the human family. It allows them to discover that they are each one of nature's greatest miracles, and that because they are, they should challenge their potential until it can be stretched no further. Being a miracle isn't enough. You must behave as one as well.

> *I am nature's greatest miracle. I am not on this earth by chance. I am here for a purpose and that purpose is to grow into a mountain, not to shrink to a grain of sand. Henceforth will I apply my efforts to become the highest mountain of all and I will strain my potential until it cries for mercy.*
>
> —Og Mandino

5

Emotional Intelligence Is Loving and Logical

Don't wish it was easier; wish you were better. Don't wish for less problems; wish for more skills. Don't wish for less challenges; wish for more wisdom.

—Jim Rohn

5
Emotional Intelligence Is Loving and Logical

What is noble can be said in any language, and what is mean should be said in none.

—Moses Ben Maimon

So what is emotional intelligence, and what does it have to do with entitlement? How do we learn to utilize it in our homes, our businesses, our schools, and our world? Let's begin by examining how emotional intelligence differs from entitlement. According to Daniel Goleman in his book *Primal Leadership: Realizing the Power of Emotional Intelligence,* emotional intelligence is concerned with two basic areas in a person's life: personal competence, which determines how we manage ourselves, and social competence, which determines how we manage relationships. Entitled people manage their personal responsibilities poorly. Instead of being personally proactive, they rely on others' resources—emotional, physical, and material—to come to their aid. This lack of personal competence negatively affects their relationships. Successful relationships rely on the personal willingness and competence of each person. The self-absorbed focus that accompanies entitlement causes people to fall short in holding up their end of relational responsibilities. A great gift to any relationship is your own personal development.

Goleman explains that emotional self-awareness is the ability to read one's own emotions and recognize their impact. It sets the stage for accurate self-assessment. "Perhaps the most telling (though least visible) sign of self-awareness is a propensity for self-reflection and thoughtfulness."[1] Entitled people spend little time in self-reflection. They have a tendency to project their shortcomings onto others.

> *I used to say, "If you will take care of me, I will take care of you." Now I say, "I will take care of me for you if you will take care of you for me."*
>
> —Jim Rohn

Self-awareness sets the stage for accurate self-assessment. It aids us in balancing our perceptions with the perceptions of others; it helps us develop confidence in ourselves, and a sound sense of our worth and capabilities. Through the development of self-awareness we strengthen and improve self-management skills. Through developing self-management skills we learn to trust ourselves. When we are able to control our feelings and impulses, we create around us an environment of safety, security, and fairness. We learn to control disruptive emotions and impulses, by learning to think before we act. Some psychologists refer to this as *response*-ability. Developing *response*-ability allows us to choose responsible actions. This simple habit of inserting conscious thought between a stimulus and a response frees us from being dominated by anger and fear.

Self-management skills play a critical role in relationships and personal achievement. They drive us to improve our personal, professional, and spiritual performance and to meet inner standards of excellence. Self-management, then, is the component of emotional intelligence that frees us from being a prisoner of our feelings, especially the feelings of anger and rage.

People who have developed emotional self-awareness and self-management skills take more initiative toward their dreams and have a better sense of their responsibility to the world around them. They are eager to take action and seize opportunities; with action and effort come optimism, hope, and happiness—all enemies of entitlement.

1. Daniel Goleman, *Primal Leadership: Realizing the Power of Emotional Intelligence*, 2002.

> *The inside-out approach says that private victories precede public victories, that making and keeping promises to ourselves precedes making and keeping promises to others. It says it is futile to put personality ahead of character, to try to improve relationships with others before improving ourselves.*
>
> —Stephen Covey

From self-awareness we grow toward social-awareness and empathy. Entitlement leaves little room for empathy in our lives; however, empathy is one of the most critical skills one can develop when learning to live a life filled with Love and Logic. Empathy is what we must express first, before anyone learns to trust our reactions. Empathy moves us to take the feelings of others into thoughtful consideration, which allows us to make intelligent choices based on those feelings.

From empathy grows sympathy. Sympathy allows us to relate to the feelings of another. It inspires a compassion that is born out of sorrow for the distress or misfortunes of others and creates within us the desire to help. This process nurtures an environment of kindness and tenderness.

Empathy inspires us to listen. Listening is a vital component of good communication, and is very different from the ability to hear. Listening requires us to choose to pay attention to what is being communicated with an open mind. Entitlement makes open, balanced communication impossible because balanced communication requires that both people have the ability to express their opinions and listen to the opinions of others. Entitled people are usually good at expressing their opinions as facts, but are shallow, disinterested listeners. It is difficult to listen when you believe that yours is the only right answer, or when you feel threatened by the question.

Win–win situations are dependent upon an individual's ability to listen carefully to all opinions and remain open to a myriad of possibilities.

People who are lost in a sense of entitlement usually believe that their way is the right way, the only way, and listening is a skill that the other person, to whom they are complaining, needs to learn. Emotional intelligence strengthens our ability to listen. It strengthens our ability to make valid, constructive points, while respectfully addressing the needs and concerns of another.

People who have never learned the skill of listening communicate from guarded and defensive positions. A defensive posture is always supported by entitlement, such as, "I don't have to stand here and listen to this garbage." A defensive posture usually escalates to anger and rage, which in turn leads to abuse. Those who purposefully harm others convince themselves that they are *entitled* to do so. Entitlement leads them to believe that others deserve to be punished, that they "have it coming." People blinded by entitlement set themselves up as judge and jury, often without the benefit of a full set of facts. They work from a self-centered agenda that makes them *right,* and therefore justified, and impairs their ability to see another's point of view.

> *Compassion and nonviolence help us to see the enemy's point of view, to hear his questions, to know his assessment of ourselves. For from his view we may indeed see the basic weakness of our own condition, and if we are mature, we may learn and grow and profit from the wisdom of the brothers who are called the opposition.*
>
> —MARTIN LUTHER KING, JR.

Self-awareness, self-management, and empathy all come together in the last domain of emotional intelligence: relationship management. Relationship management begins with personal integrity. Integrity is the cornerstone of all successful relationships. Living a life of integrity means that we are willing to *be* who we say we are, and requires that we understand accountability, which is *doing* what we say we'll do. The concept is simple and yet for most of us it's a struggle. In order for integrity to serve us, and our relationships, it must become a habit. We must be conscious of what we say, and say only what we mean.

The greatest gift we give to ourselves or anyone else is our *word,* and only we can determine its value. It is one of the greatest endowments that we can offer. Our willingness to accept personal responsibility for our lives and our actions is at the core of this gift. People living in integrity make their choices based upon their standards and values regardless of the situation. If they say they will do something, they do it. Great writers write everyday, and study other great writers. The actions of compassionate people reflect kindness and gentleness. The actions of unstoppable people reflect courage and perseverance. Words are important because they speak our values, goals, desires, and strengths. In the business world, studies tell us that integrity is the number one quality sought in every field.

> *You never know till you try to reach them how accessible men are; but you must approach each man by the right door.*
>
> —Henry Ward Beecher

Emotional intelligence teaches us how to approach, through the right door, those we wish to approach. It encourages us to listen to others with dignity and respect in an attempt to understand their point of view. It aids us in making positive choices for our lives, and combines self-management skills, integrity, and accountability to inspire us to treat other people the way we would want to be treated. It motivates us to ask one simple question before making important relational decisions: *"How would I want to be treated in this situation?"*

Keen emotional intelligence requires that we move away from an entitled perspective. Becoming aware of and then continuing to pay attention to the distinction between an entitlement and an endowment is a critical piece of emotional intelligence.

When we come from an endowed focus of life, our expectations are positive and hopeful, our conversations balanced and just. We look for the best in our relationships with people. We begin to believe in cooperation and communication.

Entitlement cripples our ability to be grateful. Just as darkness is the absence of light, entitlement is the absence of appreciation. Entitlement, together with the fear that accompanies it, limits us from seeing anything but scarcity, lack, frustration, and disappointment. It chokes the life out of hope. It shrinks our thoughts of social concern and responsibility into petty, self-serving complaints.

William Bennett tells us:

> The purpose of an education is not merely to prepare citizens for work, it is to prepare them for life—for the eminently practical tasks of living well, thinking wisely, and acting sensibly. When effectively executed, education serves not to separate but to unite the classes, endowing them with a respect for their national heritage, an appreciation for commonly shared values, and reverence for diligence, truth, and compassion. When our schools fail to fulfill this vital role, our citizens (especially those least able to learn these lessons at home) are forever diminished—and we, as a nation, are diminished as well.[2]

As human beings we base our conduct, our decisions, our work ethic, our choice of kindnesses on something, and without an emotionally intelligent influence to rely on, how do we ensure that our children develop a foundation of character and ethics upon which to grow? That is what Love and Logic techniques are about. When we put loving and logical strategies to work in our lives and we model and teach them to our children, our children develop a strong sense of self that cannot be easily broken or shaken apart. Today this is more important than ever before.

2. Special to *Hoover Digest,* 2003, adapted from a speech delivered at the Hoover Institution on May 1, 2000, by William Bennett.

Consider the following story:

I [Dawn] have a dear friend, who lives in Atlanta. She called me crying one evening. Through her tears she explained that she had just had a very difficult conversation with her two daughters, who at the time were fourteen and nine. A thirteen-year-old girl from their school had just hanged herself in her closet after reading prank e-mails from the so-called *cool* group, who decided that it would be fun to all gang up on her and tell her that she had no chance of ever being popular, and that no one liked her. Her reaction to these seemingly ridiculous e-mails was extreme. Their words cut her every bit as deeply as if they had stabbed her with knives. Because of her vulnerability, she had no capacity to gain distance on the situation, and couldn't realize that these girls were unworthy of determining her future. They were simply mean spirited, immature, self-consumed young girls that decided that they would brutalize someone more vulnerable than themselves. Entitlement had lied to them and told them that they had the right to be cruel and demeaning. Thoughtlessly they behaved in ways that no one with any emotional intelligence would allow himself or herself to behave.

6

"It's Not Fair!": Opportunity in Disguise

Opportunity often comes disguised in the form of misfortune, or temporary defeat.

—Napoleon Hill

6
"It's Not Fair!": Opportunity in Disguise

Opportunities multiply as they are seized.

—Sun Tzu

One afternoon early in his freshman year, my (Dawn's) son Corbin came home extremely upset. He was a straight-A student; in fact, in his entire school career, he had never made a B. His score in algebra was 98 percent. He was taking a test one afternoon and, a third of the way into it, his math teacher noticed that his notes were under his desk. He had slipped them there after reviewing for his test and not given them a second thought. His teacher accused him of cheating. He was devastated. With everything in him he argued his complete innocence and defended his integrity. His teacher, not appreciating what she perceived as arrogance, told him there would be no further discussion. She separated him and instructed him to complete the test, which he did.

When she graded it she discovered that he had scored just as well on the last two thirds of the test as he had on the first third, which he had completed with the notes under his desk. Corbin believed that the results had proven that he knew the material and did not need to cheat, but she had taken her stand, and was standing on principle. The notes were under his seat, even if he had not used them or needed them. She gave him a zero on the test. Not only was he was infuriated, but he was also devastated. He had never been accused of cheating before, and he had never received a zero. He was beside himself.

He came home and cried out in anger and frustration. "I can't get her to listen to me. She is completely unreasonable. Who does she think she is to accuse me?"

"She thinks that she is your teacher," I replied.

"Well, it's not fair, it's not right. What if I get my first B over something as unfair as this?" he yelled. "It's not fair, it's simply not fair!"

"Life isn't fair, but that is not the point here," I explained as I wrapped my arms around him to give him a hug. He pulled away as if to say a hug was not going to fix this. I sat him down and looked into his eyes. "There is a much greater lesson than algebra here for you to benefit from. Throughout your life, you will encounter situations that are not fair. Tragic car accidents caused by drunken drivers are not fair, cancer is not fair, working for someone who is petty, jealous, or devious is not fair, thieves breaking into your home are not fair, and no, this situation does not appear to be fair, but sweetheart, that is not the point. The point is not what happens to us, the point is in what we choose to do about what happens to us, and what kind of person we are committed to being in the process. That is the critical lesson that this situation is offering you. You have a choice here. Are you going to allow this situation to make you angry, judgmental, hostile, and frustrated? Or are you going to accept the reality of its inequity and plan your course of action. Whether it was your fault or not, it is your *responsibility* to determine how you are going to react. What do you want to do now? Who do you want to become because of this? And what story do you want to tell your children when they are struggling with a similar experience?" I asked.

"I want to tell them that I did not crater. I want to tell them that even though it was not fair, I decided to do whatever was necessary to overcome my teacher's false perception of me, to prove to myself that I can stand strong," he said with determination.

Action is a great restorer and builder of confidence. Inaction is not only the result but the cause of fear. Perhaps the action you take will be successful; perhaps different action or adjustments

> *will have to follow. But any action is better than no action at all. So don't wait for trouble to intimidate or paralyze you. Make a move.*
>
> —Norman Vincent Peale

He worked the rest of the semester to bring his grade up. He did every extra credit project that was offered, and requested more. He did extremely well on every test and homework assignment. By the end of the semester, with every effort exhausted, he had managed to bring his grade back to an 89.5 percent.

"What happens if you make a B?" I asked.

"I have no control over that anymore," he replied. "This semester has taught me a great deal about who I am. I did my best. I have no doubts about that. I am proud of my effort and I am proud that I chose to be a person that I could respect in spite of this terrible situation. I now know what I am made of, and what I am made of is good. No matter what my teacher decides to give me in algebra, I give myself an A in choice," he said with a smile.

> *Know thyself.*
>
> —Plato

The next day his teacher told him that as a reward for his dedication and determined attitude she planned to round his grade back up to the A he deserved. He learned a great deal in math class that semester, lessons that he will appreciate for the rest of his life.

Appreciation, even for the challenges we face in life, is vital to success. In our frenzied efforts to succeed quickly, we live life faster and consume more, leaving no time for appreciation. We are too tired from working nonstop in order to satisfy our accumulation addiction to notice the bounty supplied by life, left in the rain to rot.

We must awaken to the gift that appreciation brings into our homes, our schools, our businesses, and especially our hearts. As I stated previously, appreciation is a choice. It is a conscious way we choose to perceive and evaluate the status of our lives. It calls us to continually count the gifts that can become invisible, such as health, love, relationships, the kindness and charity of strangers, material blessings, and the blessings that a challenge can bring us. Often the greatest opportunities are disguised as misfortune. Only we can choose how we will use each experience.

> *We can throw stones, complain about them, stumble on them, climb over them, or build with them.*
>
> —William Arthur Ward

Opportunities, both good and bad, are gifts. If we lose sight of this fact, entitlement can cause us to mistake gifts for garbage. I (Dawn) will share a story from one of my earlier books, *Greatness and Children: Learn the Rules,* that is a perfect example:

> I had a teenage client that came to me complaining about her father. She told me that he was completely unreasonable. I will spare you her exact terminology. She had gone on a three-day weekend, out of town ski trip to Colorado. She had a wonderful time, partied, and stayed up all hours of the night. She arrived home exhausted and realized that she had not done her homework. (After all, she was having fun on a ski trip!) Her father had the gall to expect her to go to school the next day. He told her that her homework was her responsibility, not his. He explained that she knew before she left that she had assignments to do, and she also knew she would have school on Monday.
>
> The girl could not believe her father's total lack of understanding and compassion. She was furious with him. She ran to her room and slammed the door, screaming, "I hate you! You don't understand! All you care about is yourself!"

> Not only had she missed the point of the great privilege of the trip, her twisted, self-focused, entitled perspective justified her in making her father the culprit for her total lack of responsibility.
>
> "What do you owe your father for the privilege of the trip he gave you?" I asked, attempting to lead her toward the answer: gratitude.
>
> "Huh?" she replied. "I don't owe him anything. Parents are supposed to give their kids great stuff; it's their job."

It was obvious she knew very little about accountability and responsibility, and even less about appreciation.

Also in my book *Greatness and Children,* I recount a wonderful story shared by Dr. Foster Cline about taking a special trip to Stockholm:

> When the other parents and children on the trip arrived at the hotel, Dr. Cline noticed that the other twelve-year-old children were ordering their parents around. "Take my bags to the room. I'm going to go swimming with the other kids." He was amazed that the parents were scurrying around, gathering up their children's suitcases and belongings, while the children ran off to enjoy themselves.
>
> He looked at his twelve-year-old son and said, "Please take our bags to the room and when you are finished, you can join the other children. Your mother and I will be in the restaurant having a cup of coffee if you need us for anything."
>
> His son wrinkled his nose and said, "I'm glad that you have a minion to do your bidding."
>
> "A minion who was invited on this lovely trip because he is so much fun and a great deal of help. Thank you, son." With that, he turned and went to the restaurant with his wife, trusting fully that the bags would be properly delivered to the room.[1]

1. Story told by Foster Cline in a seminar in Tulsa, Oklahoma, quoted in Dawn L. Billings, *Greatness and Children: Learn the Rules,* DCB Publishing, 2003.

Notice any difference in the two stories? One child was being taught nothing of appreciation, responsibility, and accountability, the other was.

In his book *Secrets for Success and Happiness,* Og Mandino recounts:

> Samuel Taylor Coleridge was entertaining a visitor one day when the conversation got around to children. "I believe," said the visitor, "that children should be given free reign to think and act [and] thus learn at an early age to make their own decisions. That is the only way they can grow to their full potential."
>
> Coleridge interrupted the man and said, "I would like you to see my flower garden," and the poet led the man outside. The visitor took one look and exclaimed, "Why that is nothing but a yard full of weeds!"
>
> "Well," smiled Coleridge, "it was filled with roses, but this year I thought I would let the garden grow as it willed without my tending to it. And you can see the results."[2]

Hearts and minds are like gardens. We must tend them, cultivate them, and feed them. Happiness and success come when we understand the rich endowments that life offers us, and when we choose to be responsible for using these endowments to benefit others. Accountability, responsibility, and appreciation, like sun, water, and good soil, cause happiness and success to grow in all areas of our lives. The only way we can know how rich we are is to continually count our blessings. When we miss opportunities to be appreciative and to collaborate with each other, we fail. Entitled attitudes, like weeds, not only are unattractive, but they also bring nothing of value to anyone's life.

> *The mind is a bit like a garden. If it isn't fed and cultivated, weeds will take it over.*
>
> —Erwin G. Hall

2. Og Mandino, *Secrets for Success and Happiness,* Ballantine Books, 1995.

7

The Courage to Say No, the Joy of Saying Yes, and the Wisdom to Know the Difference

Wealth stays with us a little moment
if at all: only our characters are
steadfast, not our gold.

—Euripides

7

The Courage to Say No, the Joy of Saying Yes, and the Wisdom to Know the Difference

By the time we realize our parents were right, we have children who think we're wrong.

—Guillermo Hernandez

Entitlement is complicated but avoiding it is simple. Notice that we did not say *easy.* We said *simple.* It takes courage and a belief that character is more important than a façade. Some parents are more concerned about their child's grade-point average than they are about his or her character. While one is a charcoal mark on a piece of paper that fades easily over time, the other is a mark of courage that presses itself into every action a person chooses for the rest of his or her life.

Jim tells a very thought-provoking story about a mother caught in a struggle that had her terribly confused and was tearing her heart apart. It seems that her son came home from school one day and confessed that he had missed six days of school. When she asked what he meant by "missed," he simply winked at her. His mother was very concerned because she knew the school rules: six unexcused absences meant a student would automatically flunk their course and have to retake it at a later time. She asked her son how he was going to fit in the time required to retake the course. He looked at her somewhat surprised and answered, "I'm not going to have to take the course over again because the absences were not *really* unexcused."

"What do you mean they weren't *really* unexcused?" the mother asked.

"You know ... ," the son said, as if letting her in on a trade secret.

"You forged my name to excuse slips?" the mother continued.

"Mom, I'm an honor student. I can't flunk a course because of unexcused absences. I would no longer be an honor student. You can't tell anyone about this. I know you understand that. Besides, the only reason that I told you is because I knew that I could trust you to understand. I expect you to honor our parent-child confidentiality."

Can you imagine how you would feel as a parent if your child was having this conversation with you? You would be talking to an honor student with no honor. How would you handle this situation? Would you be the parent who said ...

> Wow son, how very sad. I am so sorry that your choices have put you in this difficult predicament. How are you going to tell the school the truth and resolve this situation so that your character and honor remain intact? I love you very much and believe in the kind of person you are. I can't lie in this situation. If I did I would give up a piece of my honor and then neither of us would be able to maintain respect for me. Let me know how you would like me to support you in resolving this with integrity because to me you are a student with great honor and I can treat you as nothing less.

or ...

> I can't believe you have put me in this situation. How could you sign my name to a lie? You know better than this! I have raised you better than this! What would my friends think if they knew the truth? I thought I could trust you but just look at you. You should be ashamed. I have no choice but to lie for you this time, but this is the last time, do you hear me? I won't do this again. I have had it with your little charades and will not tolerate this again. Do you hear me?

There was a mother who had a fifteen-and-a-half-year-old son who was a champion of a boy. Because he was doing so well in school and with his responsibilities around the house, his mother wanted to do something special for him to reward his good decisions. She asked the son what he might like and he told her that his very nice girlfriend had never been to a Broadway play and asked if the mother would purchase tickets for her to take them to see *The Producers*. The mother called and ordered tickets. The afternoon of the play, around five o'clock, a friend of the mother's called to check in and say hello. The mother explained that she was getting ready to take her son and his girlfriend out to dinner and to a Broadway play that evening. "Wonderful," said the friend. "Which play are you going to see?"

"*The Producers*," replied the mother.

"That really surprises me," her friend said, knowing the mother very well.

"Why?" asked the mom.

"Well, we went to see it when we were in New York and walked out within the first fifteen minutes because of the profanity."

"What profanity?" the mother questioned.

"That play would have been wonderful and clever but there is so much profanity that it didn't fit our value system, so we chose to leave."

"You are kidding me," the mother replied, completely shocked at what her friend was telling her.

The mother quickly hung up the phone and rushed to get her paper. She had been told that there was a large article about the play. As she read through the article she read nothing about the profanity that her friend had spoken about, but she noticed the small letters in the advertisement: "*for mature audiences only*." By this time it was 6:30 and her son's girlfriend had arrived at their home. "*What am I going to do now*," she thought. She could hardly bear the thought of embarrassing her son, but she knew that she could not take him and his girlfriend to a play that she believed might go against her personal values. She had been a strong proponent of parents taking an active role in limiting the junk that children can be exposed to by television, movies, music, and video games. How could she hold her value system intact and stand for what she believed if she were to take these two young people to this play? She couldn't. She went to her son and his girlfriend and explained what she had just learned. She was very distressed, but her son was even more so.

"You've got to be kidding, Mom? This play has won numerous awards. It is a comedy, so you don't have to take the language seriously. You are being unreasonable, old-fashioned, and overprotective. How could you embarrass me like this? How could you promise to do something and then go back on your word? It is not fair. It isn't as bad as you think."

The mother asked her son if he knew anything about the play, and he told her yes, that he had researched it on the Internet.

"Then tell me about the profanity. You know me. Would it be something that I would have purchased tickets to if I knew?"

"Maybe not," the son said as he defended the play. "They use a lot of cuss words, but don't pay attention to that part. It is no big deal. We hear them all of the time on the television, in movies, at school. They are everywhere."

"They are not in my home. We don't have HBO, or Cinemax, and we are careful about what we watch on television in our home. Why would I pay a large sum of money for you to be exposed to language that I do not believe should be said in front of you and especially in front of a young woman that you care about? Son, there was a time when if a man heard those words said in front of a lady, he would fight to the death for her honor."

"Mom, what world do you live in? Do you hear yourself? We don't live in those times. We live here, now. This world is different. We are desensitized to words like that," he argued passionately.

"Well, I'm not," responded his mother. "Nor do I plan to be."

"This is ridiculous! You are ruining this for me. How could you do this?" her son continued to argue.

"I can do it because I love you. I can do it because I must stand for what I believe in because if I don't, it would be hard for you to respect me and take me seriously. I love you son. I have a responsibility to you. I have a responsibility to your girlfriend, whose parents have put her in my care for this evening. But most of all, I have a responsibility to my heartfelt values. I cannot violate who I am, and what I believe in, simply to accommodate your anger at my decision. I will take you to a marvelous dinner and I promise to make this up to you. I will keep my word and take you to a wonderful Broadway play when the next one comes that does not ask me to violate my values. I hope that you will understand, but even if you don't, I must be consistent with who I believe I am, and what I believe that I stand for."

The son was quiet most of the evening. His anger was just under the surface all night. He glared at his mother and really struggled with her decision. Three weeks later he went to a leadership seminar, where he had to create a platform that he felt strongly about that he believed would make a positive difference in the world. The platform he chose was to clean up television programs during prime family viewing times, when children could be watching. He designed a plan that would help protect children from unnecessary profanity, sex, and violence during prime-time evening hours. When he returned home it was Mother's Day. He made a wonderful movie for his mom set to music, in which he included his own poetry and tribute mixed in with pictures of himself from the time he was a baby until the present. The theme of the movie was "Thank you for having the courage to say NO in the face of distress, as well as the joy of saying YES when it was for the best in a person." It was hard for the mother to watch the movie through her tears. She had never received a gift so wonderful.

It is never easy to take a stand, especially an unpopular one. It takes courage and a belief in the long-term positive impact of your decisions. But as parents, we will be called upon to make unpopular decisions for long-term benefits because our children cannot have the depth of vision that we have for them.

Character develops itself in the stream of life.

—Johann Wolfgang von Goethe

Do you know any parents who are more concerned about their kid's grade-point average than they are about his or her character? Go to your local school and visit with the teachers and they will tell you that they are facing a national epidemic of parents who will do anything they can to make sure their kids look good to the outside world. Would you guess that these parents are willing to lie for their kids, do their homework for them, and intimidate teachers into giving their children better grades than they have earned?

If their child is lazy about doing their homework, these parents have a tendency to blame the teacher. If their child does not train hard enough to earn a place as a starter on the football, basketball, or baseball team, for example, these parents blame the coach. If their child is arrested for a crime, these same parents find ways to excuse the dishonest or harmful action of their child and instead blame the police.

We know that if you are still reading this book, you want your children to become people who have great character to guide them, but how do we help them to develop and strengthen their character? Actually, that is the easy part. Life will develop and strengthen their character. We must simply have the commitment to stay out of life's way. It takes real courage to say no. Many parents want to say yes. Saying yes is easier. It is more fun. It is pleasing and brings no wrath with it. But it is not always the answer that is best for our children to hear.

So how do we learn when to say yes and when to say no, and more important, how do we develop the internal and external fortitude to stand by it when we choose to say it? One of the first things we must do is build a support team of like-minded parents. Yes, this means moving away from toxic parents, and this may mean stepping out of your private fortress and developing meaningful relationships with other people who have children. In our society there are people who do not know their neighbors, the friends of their children, or the friends of their parents; in fact, they do not know anyone they are not forced to come in contact with through their work or church activities. Building a support team requires that we step outside of our normal comfort zone and take the action necessary not only to build but also to maintain relationships with other like-minded parents.

The next important step in developing and strengthening our courage is to enlist the support of the school that our children are attending. We need to let the school know what we are working on with our children. The school needs to understand the values that we are attempting to impart to our children at a particular time. Not only does this help us, but it also helps the teachers and is especially important for our children. The more consistency we can offer them, the easier it is for them to learn and adapt to that to which we want them to adapt. If you communicate to a teacher what your needs are, he or she has a much better chance of complying. Sad but true, many teachers have become gun-shy. They have been intimidated so often that they may need a written statement of your intentions to support them to do what is right for your child.

The next important skill to develop in order to combat entitlement is the skill of dealing with the argumentative side of your children. Children, like us, love to argue. They want their way. It is our job as parents to give it to them only when it benefits them and serves their higher good. With Love and Logic techniques we can actually begin to make handling these once stressful experiences fun.

It is our job as parents to help our children learn the difference between wants and needs. This means that your child, who is naturally a bundle of wants, will often be mad or disappointed that you are not quick to give in.

One of the most valuable tools you need to help you remain strong in the face of demands, complaints, guilt, and temper tantrums is the following sentence (write it on your finger or keep it on the tip of your tongue):

"I LOVE YOU TOO MUCH TO ARGUE ABOUT THAT."

For example:

CHILD: "I really need a TV in my room so I can watch what I want. All my friends have them. I don't know why you're so selfish."

PARENT: (with sincere empathy) "Sweetie, I love you too much to argue about that." (And then walk away.)

Any self-respecting kid won't give up this easy, of course. Don't expect that yours will. Be prepared to use what we affectionately call the ***Broken Record*** technique:

CHILD: "This is so lame. It's not going to cost you that much to show that you care about me for once!"
PARENT: (again with sincere empathy) "So ... what did I say?"

Effective parents don't try to match wits with a child who has nothing to lose by badgering. These parents simply keep repeating with sincere empathy, "So ... what did I say?"

Remember that this technique is not designed to make children happy. It is designed to help them understand the boundaries that you have determined are best for them and your family. Some parents ask, "What if the child gets mad?" Well, our recommendation is that you attempt to allow yourself to become pleased with yourself, because in most cases the child becoming angry and frustrated means that the technique is working. Have courage. By all means, don't give up. Remember, your job is not to provide your children immediate happiness. It is to provide your children with long-term success, which will bring them a real sense of joy by allowing them to live a life filled with responsibility, character, and appreciation. As we learn to truly appreciate the value of actually earning what we want, we build self-worth. It is not what we get in life that is valuable, that truly makes the difference, but what we become.

How to Say No When You Know You Should, But Can't Explain Why

The "I'm Not Ready for That Yet" *Technique*

DAUGHTER: "Rick—you know, Mom, that really cute guy in my social studies class—wants me to go out with him."
MOM: "Well, Sweetie, I don't know.
DAUGHTER: "Come on, Mom. I'm thirteen. My friends are already dating. You don't need to keep treating me like a baby."
MOM: "Well, Sweetie, I'm just not ready for you to be dating."
DAUGHTER: "Why not. I'm a good girl. I get good grades. This is so

	lame. All the other parents let their daughters date. You're so old-fashioned."
MOM:	"I don't know why I'm not ready, but I'm not.
DAUGHTER:	"Well you should be."
MOM:	"I bet it looks that way to you, but I'm just not ready."
DAUGHTER:	"That's stupid."
MOM:	"I'm sure it looks that way, but I love you too much to argue with you. If it helps, you can tell Rick that I'm a dinosaur, and totally unreasonable, and that it's not your fault that I'm not ready for you to date. See ya, Sweetie."

8

A.C.T. Now to Inoculate Your Kids Against the Wrath of Entitlement

A coach is someone who tells you what you don't want to hear, who has you see what you don't want to see, so you can be who you have always known you could be.

—Tom Landry

8

A.C.T. Now to Inoculate Your Kids Against the Wrath of Entitlement

What the vast majority of American children need is to stop being pampered, stop being indulged, stop being chauffeured, stop being catered to. In the final analysis it is not what you do for your children but what you have taught them to do for themselves that will make them successful human beings.

—Ann Landers

This is the chapter that will encourage you to A.C.T. now to inoculate your kids against the wrath of entitlement. Here we will provide you with actual templates for handling various situations with your children. We have described in great detail the negative effects entitlement has on your children's lives. Now it is time for us to supply you with some commonsense, well-thought-out, loving yet logical techniques that can help you combat the entitlement that threatens the happiness and success of your children.

The acronym "A.C.T." will remind you that being successful at raising responsible, happy children requires three important things—**Attitude**, **Courage**, and **Techniques**. You will be responsible for developing and maintaining the right attitude of empathy and love, as well as supplying yourself the courage to maintain your consistency and follow through. What we will happily add to the mix are powerful, effective, proven techniques that will make your experience as a parent, teacher, grandparent, or caregiver in any capacity much more satisfying and rewarding. These techniques have been carefully designed and researched over many years. They have proven their effectiveness in homes across the nation, and will help you help your children in developing the necessary skills that will enable them to make powerful, positive choices in their lives.

So let's begin with the two basic rules of Love and Logic.

Rule #1: Adults set firm limits in loving ways without anger, lecture, or threats.

Threats and warnings are extremely ineffective. Threats simply give children an opportunity to brace and fortify themselves. They set children up and invite them to test the resolve of the threat-giver. They give children time to think of ways to violate a rule in a slightly different way and allow them to argue about fairness. Threats also orchestrate arguments and give a child time to figure out a way to triangulate a situation in their attempt to defend their position and manipulate you into conceding to their desired outcome. Threats also can create a perception of control loss, and often this perception becomes the dominant issue instead of the original issue at hand. The perception of loss of control stimulates manipulative and resistant behaviors. Warnings and threats not only do not work, but also work against your desired outcome.

So what do you do instead of issuing threats and warnings? Wise parents state expectations and then back them up. Children growing up in homes where expectations are clear and the consequences are consistent and dependable are more secure. Children growing up in homes where parents are consistently courageous and loving in their parenting styles know from experience that violations of rules result in consequences. Even if these children don't know which exact consequence to expect, they know, beyond a shadow of a doubt, that the parents will think of something and follow through.

PARENT: "Jeremy, we will be expecting you to be home for dinner at six o'clock. Thanks, see you later pal."

JEREMY: "I don't want to come home that early. What's going to happen if I don't?"

PARENT: "Oh, I'll think of something."

JEREMY: "What?"

PARENT: "You worry too much. I'll figure it out if I need to. Try not to worry. See you at six."

Wise parents know the tremendous value of the word "something." Love and Logic parents cherish the phrase "I'll think of something." Their children know this phrase well, and also know that it is never a good idea to leave it up to the parent to choose.

Granted, there are times when children need the advice of older, wiser people regarding the possible outcomes of their decisions. People who choose to parent out of a Love and Logic style of parenting are not afraid to offer this kind of advice. However, since these parents understand that threats are often seen as challenges by their children, they make sure that their advice is not shared in the form of a threat.

A Simple Love and Logic Advice Technique

Step 1: The parent does not say, "Don't do that." Instead, the parent talks about what he or she would or would not do: "Oh, I don't think I would do that."

Step 2: The parent describes how the consequences might affect him or her personally: "If I did that, this is what might happen to *me*." (At this time, the parent thinks to him- or herself, "Please let this go wrong for the child if he doesn't take my advice. I'm going to look foolish if he makes a bad decision and it goes well.")

Step 3: The parent most likely stands back and watches with interest and curiosity. Why? The child is probably not taking the parent's advice.

Step 4: The parent is available to provide empathy and sadness for the child if the situation does not go well for him or her.

DAD: "Oh, I don't think I'd go out there and smart-mouth those bigger kids. If I did that, I'd probably get a fat lip, or a bloody nose, or have to carry my tooth around in an envelope for a week."

Dad watches with interest and curiosity as his son disregards his valuable advice. At this moment, are you thinking that there are some kids out there who will give this child some "on-the-job training" about controlling his mouth? If so, you're right.

And how is this training going to take place? Will it be with words, or violent action? You're right again. However, right at the time the other kid retaliates, there will be a flash of recognition in the son's mind: "Wow! This is exactly what my dad said would happen. He must really be wise. Maybe I better listen to him next time."

Now, how is he greeted when he comes back into the home? Some parents would feel a need to say, "I told you so. You never listen. I hope this teaches you a good lesson!" You know that this will do nothing but rub salt in the wound.

A parent who chooses to utilize Love and Logic techniques provides sincere empathy. Empathy shows love, but also helps lock in the lesson: "Boy oh boy look at that lip. That's what happens to me when I mouth off to bigger, stronger people. Let me give you a hug and let's get some ice for that lip." Love and empathy drive home life's important lessons in ways that sarcastic *"I told you so's"* can never do.

Rule #2: When a child causes a problem, the adult hands it back in loving ways.

1. In a loving way, the adult holds the child accountable for solving his or her problems in a way that does not make a problem for others.

There is no greater teacher than experience, and we gain no greater experience than when we are faced with natural, logical consequences from poor choices. But what if you do hold your children responsible for their actions and they end up seeing you as being mean or they decide that you are the source of their problems? What good will that do? The truth of the matter is that it will make things worse. Love and Logic parenting offers you the secret to holding kids accountable for their actions without them seeing you as being mean:

Lock in empathy before talking about consequences.

If you want your child to see you as being mean, do it this way:

Parent: "What's the matter with you? I told you to be careful, but you never listen. Now you've wrecked the car and you're going to have to pay for the damage before you drive again!"

Teen: "You don't understand. It was an accident. It's not my fault. You make me drive that crummy old car. If you gave me a decent car I wouldn't be ..."

This youngster is now defensive, and sees the parent as the source of his problem. Surely he is giving very little thought to his role in the situation, and is learning little from the consequence.

If you'd rather have your child see his or her own behavior as the source of the problem, do it this way:

Parent: "Oh, no. I bet you feel awful. It's not easy being a new driver. I'm so glad you're not hurt. But don't worry. You'll be driving again as soon as you get the repairs paid for. Let me know how you want to handle that."

2. The child is offered choices with limits.

Children must learn how to make good choices. Learning to make good choices is like learning everything else: all new skills must be repeated and practiced.

All people, large or small, have a strong need for control. This natural need is so strong that people will do anything, and we mean *anything*, to feel in control. Parents who remember that their kids will either get control on their parent's terms, or take it on their own terms, appreciate the value of giving kids lots of choices. Please don't jump to the opinion that we should allow kids unlimited choices and control. Love and Logic parents offer choices within limits that are appropriate for the age of their child.

There are several rules to remember when providing choices:

- Give choices before a child says no.
- Give two choices, either of which will make you happy. When a kid has a choice between one option the parent likes and one the parent doesn't, the kid usually picks the one the parent doesn't like.
- Give your child no more than ten seconds to decide. If no decision is made, you make the choice.
- Give choices that don't affect anyone other than the child.
- Give lots of little choices, and give them when you are happy and when it is easy to think of them. Trying to think of choices under stress is nearly impossible for most parents.
- Parents who give lots of little choices can gain a lot of control when they need it by saying, "Wait a minute. Don't I usually let you decide whenever I can? Now it's my turn to decide. Thanks for understanding."

KIDS MAKE THE LITTLE DECISIONS, PARENTS MAKE THE BIG ONES.

3. The adult uses enforceable statements.

Enforceable statements, such as those exampled below and later in this chapter, will aid you in changing the way you structure your sentences, so you can strengthen their effectiveness as well as deliver them with empathy and calm.

Unenforceable: "Hurry up!" (regardless of how it is said)
Enforceable: "My car is leaving in five minutes."

Unenforceable: "You show a little respect, young lady."
Enforceable: "I'll be glad to listen when your voice sounds like mine."

Unenforceable: "As long as you live in this house, you are not going to drink."
Enforceable: "I'll be glad to let you drive my car as long as I never have to worry about alcohol."

4. The adult provides delayed or extended consequences.

Most parents labor under an incorrect assumption. They believe that consequences delivered immediately have a more powerful and salient impact. This is not true. It is far better for parents to handle a misbehaving youngster by saying, "I'm going to have to do something about that behavior, but not right now. Give me some time to think about it. I'll get back to you on this." It is helpful to add, "Try not to worry about it."

What are the benefits of this?

- The parent has time to calm down and think of the best way to handle the situation. This way the dignity of both the adult and the child can be maintained.
- The parent has time to consult with friends or experts to find the best consequence.
- The parent has time to plug any holes in the plan, getting whatever support necessary.
- The parent has time to rehearse how to lock in their empathy before stating the consequence.
- The child may stew about the problem and will probably live out several consequences in his or her mind while waiting.

5. The adult "locks in" the empathy before delivering the consequence.

Displaying empathy—genuine, heartfelt empathy—is critical when raising children to lead empowered, happy, responsible lives.

The Love and Logic Game Plan for Parents

Step 1: Maintain a positive relationship around your child's strengths and interests.

"I noticed you like to skateboard."

Research clearly shows that the primary element contributing to success with kids, especially challenging kids, is a positive relationship between the child and the adults in his or her life. The research also indicates that this relationship is developed most effectively when the adults set firm limits while showing sincere interest in what is unique or special about the child. That is, this relationship blossoms when the adults notice and accept the youngster as a unique human being—and the adults maintain high expectations for the youth's behavior.

We will share with you a one-sentence intervention that has proven to be extremely successful in both home and school settings. It is called the ***"I've noticed that"*** intervention:

1. What are the child's nonacademic strengths and interests? What is special about this child?
2. List six brief statements you can use to notice these strengths and interests. (Example: "I've noticed that you really like to draw.")

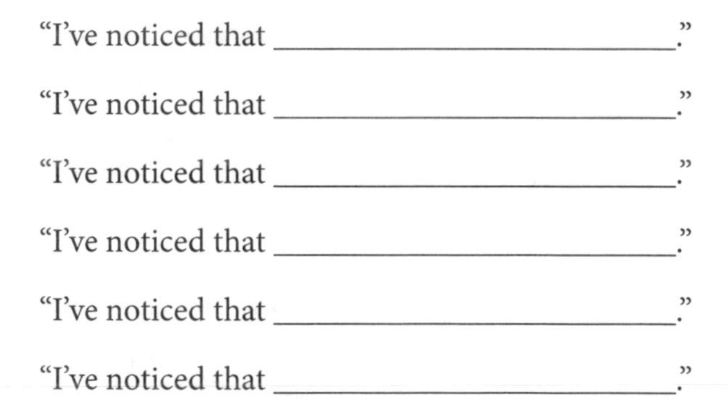
"I've noticed that ____________________________."

"I've noticed that ____________________________."

"I've noticed that ____________________________."

"I've noticed that ____________________________."

"I've noticed that ____________________________."

"I've noticed that ____________________________."

Do not end the statement with something like, "... and that's great!"

3. Pay attention to when and where you can make these statements without embarrassing the child.
4. Which other adults (or other children) will help you use this technique with the child?
5. Approach the child, smile, and use the statements identified above at least two times a week for at least three weeks.

6. Listen to the child if he or she wants to talk about the strength of interest.
7. ***Do not use this technique when the child is upset.*** Save it for calm times.
8. When the child is about to do something you don't want, or if you want him or her to do something else, experiment with saying, "Will you do this just for me?"

Step 2: Greet your child each day and evening with positives instead of negatives.

"Great to see you!" (Instead of,
"Do you have any homework?")

Most of the choices we make in our lives are based on our emotions. Most of us like to believe that our decisions are well thought out, practical, based on logic, and above all, objective. Most often they are born out of our emotions. This is neither good nor bad, it just is. It is simply how we are hard-wired. There are basically two emotions that drive the choices we make: fear and love. We can usually discern if a particular reaction is motivated by fear, and all of the emotions that are attached to fear (anger, frustration, confusion, rage, a need to dominate, etc.), or by love and its attendant emotions (compassion, joy, calm, a need to connect, etc.) simply by looking at the statements we make. Statements made out of love are usually considered positive and statements made out of fear are usually classified as negative. Let's take the examples above. *"Great to see you!"* obviously comes from love. Our approach is positive. We feel an eagerness to connect, appreciate, enjoy, and celebrate. *"Do you have any homework?"* stems from fear. It can be received by the child as negative because within the question can hide an underlying concern, born out of fear, that the child will not be responsible for their studies, either because we are afraid they will not remember to do their work on their own, because we are afraid they possibly do not care enough to complete their tasks, or because we are afraid they will stubbornly resist doing their schoolwork.

> *There is perhaps nothing so bad and so dangerous in life as fear.*
>
> —Jawaharlal Nehru

The delightful classic movie *It's a Wonderful Life* is a remarkable example of how a perspective, whether positive or negative, can powerfully affect the choices that we make. The movie did not fare well as a box office release, but now it is the most consistently watched movie in the history of feature films. The movie opens with the main character, played by Jimmy Stewart, contemplating suicide. He is burnt out, perceives himself as a failure, and believes the world would be better off without him. For the entire first half of the movie we witness his choices impacted by his fear. He needs a miracle to save him and he gets it. Through the course of the movie, he is transformed from a totally depressed, suicidal individual into a man running through the streets of his town filled with appreciation and ecstasy for life. How did this miracle occur? He started viewing his life from a completely different perspective. No facts were changed. The only change necessary in order for his life to feel totally transformed was that he change his negative approach to his relationships and circumstances and replace it with a positive one instead. Greet your children and your life with a positive perspective and you too will witness a wonderful difference.

The happiest families I know subscribe to the "Thirty-Minute Rule." No questions or complaining are allowed during the first thirty minutes when families see each other at the end of the day. This is difficult for some people to imagine. "What do you do, if you don't ask questions?" they ask.

You spend time simply enjoying each other's company without the usual questions, like:

"How was your day?"

"Where is your homework?"

"What did you do today?"

"Why didn't you call?"

This certainly doesn't mean that people aren't allowed to share their experiences of the day. Sure they are, if they want to and are excited about something. What this technique protects against is one of the family members *feeling attacked* or *feeling pounced upon* when they walk through the door.

Family members who subscribe to this rule seem to find wonderful things to do during this time, such as enjoying a snack, riding bikes, walking, or just sitting beside each other in a comfortable manner.

Step 3: Use empathy as a tool for preventing resentment and power struggles.

"What a drag. How are you going to pay for that window?"

There are so many benefits that come with developing genuine empathy in our relationships. Feeling and displaying empathy helps those we love experience the fact that we love them. Consequences delivered with empathy have powerful teaching results, and that is exactly what we hope consequences will do—teach. Some benefits to delivering consequences with empathy are:

- The child is not distracted by the adult's anger.
- The child must "own" his or her pain rather than blaming it on the adult.
- The adult-child relationship is maintained.
- The child is much less likely to seek revenge.
- The adult is seen as being able to handle problems without breaking a sweat.
- The child learns through modeling to use empathy with others.
- Lessons learned this way have lasting results.

Some Examples of Empathetic Responses

"This must really hurt, and ______________________." (Fill in the consequence.)

"This is so sad, and ______________________."

"What a bummer, and ______________________."

"How sad that you made the choice you made and that it is causing you pain, and ______________________."

Keep Your Empathy Simple and Repetitive

Most adults find it difficult to deliver empathy when a child has misbehaved. It is not our most natural reaction. Therefore, rather than getting complicated, it's easier to pick just one empathic response you can use each time you do discipline. When kids hear these same statements repeated, they learn two things:

1. This adult (my parent, teacher, etc.) cares about me.
2. This adult is not going to back down. No use in arguing the point.

Don't worry that using the exact same empathetic response will come across as redundant. People in our culture are so starved for empathy that they don't seem to recognize the words as much as their feeling upon hearing them.

Try to Find a Response You Already Know

It's always easier to use an empathic statement that you have already heard or used. A rancher in one of my (Jim's) conferences said that his father used to say, in a sad tone of voice, "*Dang, and* ________________." Find a word or saying that fits you and your children. The possibilities are endless! You can find many different suggestions at the Love and Logic website, www.loveandlogic.com.

The Power of Nonverbal Communication

Do not underestimate the power of nonverbal communication. Studies estimate that 70–90 percent of what we communicate, we do without words through subtle, nonverbal gestures. Research also reveals that children are experts at decoding these nonverbal cues. It won't work just to become a parrot of what sound like empathic responses. You must mean what you say so that the child you are communicating with feels the truth of it.

WHEN DELIVERING EMPATHIC RESPONSES,
THE DELIVERY IS AS IMPORTANT AS YOUR ACTUAL
WORDS—AVOID SARCASM AT ALL COSTS!

Step 4: Focus heavily on creating healthy beliefs about achievement.

"You got an A on that spelling test.
How did you do that?"

For almost three decades, research has shown that low achievers tend to attribute both their successful experiences and their unsuccessful experiences to uncontrollable causes—such as luck, ease or difficulty of the task, lack of intelligence, and so forth. In contrast, high achievers more often attribute their successful and unsuccessful experiences to a controllable cause—effort or a lack of it.

How do these attributions affect behavior? Simply stated, when one attributes outcomes to uncontrollable causes, why try? Is it any surprise that low-achieving children place such a low emphasis on effort, practice, and completing homework? In contrast, when one attributes outcomes to one's own behavior, it seems quite logical to work hard and practice.

Changing unhealthy attribution beliefs is a slow but essential process, requiring the following steps:

1. Write three healthy attribution beliefs on note cards.

   "I worked hard."

   "I kept trying."

   "I've been practicing."

2. Focus on noticing what he child has done well.

   "You got that problem correct."

   "You sat still through dinner."

   Do not say, "That's great!" Praise will often backfire with low achievers.

3. Ask the child to provide an explanation for their success.

   "How did you do that?"

4. Ask the child to repeat the attribution belief (from the first step) responsible for their success. Smile, point at the belief note cards, and ask, "Which one?"

   Note: It is essential that the child say the words, instead of hearing them. Why? Speaking them locks in the belief as one's own.

WHAT I SAY, I WILL SOON COME TO BELIEVE.

Step 5: Replace lectures and warnings with enforceable statements.

"I provide allowance to kids who treat me with respect."

It is important that you care enough to turn your words into gold by learning the art of enforceable statements in your home. We list here some of the most common ineffective statements used by most parents and follow them with Love and Logic enforceable statements that really work:

Ineffective: "Quit playing with your food."
Effective: "Feel free to return to the table when you can eat like the rest of us."

Ineffective: "Please be quiet. I can't listen to your brother when you are both talking at the same time."
Effective: "I'll be glad to listen to you as soon as your brother has finished talking to me."

Ineffective: "Clean your room so we can go shopping."
Effective: "I'll be happy to take you shopping as soon as your room is clean."

Ineffective: "I'm not going to play ball with you until all of you are quiet."
Effective: "I'll be happy to play ball with you as soon as you have finished talking."

Ineffective: "Don't talk while I'm reading to you."
Effective: "I will start reading to you again as soon as you have finished talking."

Ineffective: "You can't go play until you have finished your homework."
Effective: "Feel free to go play as soon as you have finished your homework."

Ineffective: "Don't shout at me!"
Effective: "I listen to people who do not yell at me."

Ineffective: "Pay attention."
Effective: "I'll start again as soon as I know you are with me."

Ineffective: "Don't be bothering your sister."
Effective: "You are welcome to stay with us as long as you are not bothering your sister."

Ineffective: "Keep your hands to yourself."
Effective: "Feel free to stay with us when you can keep your hands to yourself."

Ineffective: "Do your chores on time or you'll be grounded."
Effective: "I'll be happy to let you go with your friends as soon as your chores are finished."

Ineffective: "Don't talk to me in that tone of voice!"
Effective: "I'll listen as soon as your voice is as calm as mine."

Ineffective: "Don't be disrespectful to me!"
Effective: "I'll be glad to discuss this when I feel that appropriate respect is shown."

Ineffective: "I'm not picking up your dirty clothes."
Effective: "I'll be glad to wash the clothes that are put in the laundry room."

Ineffective: "Don't come home late from school or else."
Effective: "I drive to practice those who arrive home on time."

Ineffective: "Keep your room clean."
Effective: "All owners of neat rooms are welcome to join us for ice cream."

Ineffective: "I'm not loaning you any more money."
Effective: "I loan money to those who have collateral."

Ineffective: "If you can't remember your pencil, you're just going to have to do without."
Effective: "Feel free to borrow from anyone but me."

Ineffective: "You're not going to stay in this group and act like that."
Effective: "You may stay with us if you can give up that behavior."

Ineffective: "You're not going out without your coat."
Effective: "You may go out as soon as you have your coat."

Ineffective: "Quit breaking the rules of the game."
Effective: "Those who can follow the rules are welcome to play the game."

Ineffective: "Get this room cleaned up right now, and I mean it!"
Effective: "You are welcome to join us for _____ as soon as your room is clean."

Ineffective: "Stop arguing with me."
Effective: "I'll be glad to discuss this with you as soon as the arguing stops."

Ineffective: "Don't drink and drive."
Effective: "I loan car keys when I don't have to worry about drinking and driving."

Ineffective: "EAT!"
Effective: "I serve dinner until 7:30. Get what you need to hold you to breakfast."

Step 6: Become a master of neutralizing arguments.

"I love you too much to argue."

Living from an entitled perspective causes us to be argumentative. When we want what we want, when we want it, we feel entitled to insist on our desires. This is the beginning of all arguing. When you use Love and Logic, you neutralize arguments in a respectful and loving way while fortifying the values upon which you base your life.

Step 7: Teach your child to make regular contributions to the family (e.g., chores) without reminders.

> *"I love you too much to nag and remind you about helping. I hired someone else to do it. How are you going to pay that person?"*

Contributions fulfill the basic emotional need to be needed and to be an equally important member of the family. Contributions give children the gift of struggle, while showing them that hard work and accomplishment are personally rewarding. Contributions teach children there is no such thing as a free meal, and that earned meals actually taste better.

Techniques for Training Resistant Children to Make Contributions Without Reminders

1. Pick two contributions you are sure your child won't make.

   "Sweetie? Would you rather clean the garage of mow the yard?"

2. Don't say, "Do it now." Buy yourself time by giving a deadline.

   "Don't do it right away. Just have it done by Sunday at 6:00 P.M."

3. If your child gets defiant, delay the consequence.

   "I love you too much to argue. I'll take care of it."

4. Hope and pray your child either forgets or refuses (so you aren't tempted to nag or remind).

5. Instead of reminding, do it for your child or pay someone else to do it.

"Remember when I said that I love your too much to fight with you about doing the lawn? I had Joe from next door do it instead."

6. Ask your child how he or she plans to pay you or that other person.

   "Joe's coming over in an hour. He'll be asking you how you plan to pay him the twenty dollars."

7. If your child gets defiant, repeat step 3.

   "I love you too much to argue. I'll take care of it."

8. If you child refuses, be prepared to play "hardball" in a loving way.

   "This is unfortunate. To pay Joe, I had to pawn the bike I bought you."

   or ...

   "I'll be happy to do all the things I do around here when I don't have to worry about you making contributions to the family."

Step 8: Use delayed consequences to buy yourself time and to prevent "explosions."

> *"I'm going to have to do something about this ... but not now—later. Try not to worry about it."*

Step 9: Teach your child to delay gratification.

> *"I will address your important issue ten minutes from now, when the time is more appropriate for me and I can give you my full attention."*

Entitled people have many things in common. One of these is their inability to delay gratification. They believe that they "deserve" what they want. They even convince themselves that they are being reasonable in their requests. A seventeen-year-old girl refused her new Suzuki car that her parents purchased for her because it wasn't cool enough for her to drive. Her parents took a mortgage on their home to purchase her a Mustang, which the young woman deemed more suitable to her needs. She totaled the Mustang in less than a month, only to find a newer Mustang to replace it. Bored with her newer Mustang she decided that what she really wanted was an SUV, but only a Lexus or Cadillac Escalade would do. She showed no appreciation for her designer clothes and shoes, and refused to help her mother carry heavy bags of groceries because she thought it might make her appear as though she were less affluent. She had no concern that her parents had taken out a second mortgage on their home to supply her insatiable wants, and her response when questioned was, "They are the parents. It's their job to buy me stuff." Keep in mind she was a C grade-point student and made not one contribution to the world other than supporting the designer stores where she insisted on shopping. Still seventeen, she was expecting her fourth car and a plasma screen television for a graduation present, all the while knowing her parents were in serious financial jeopardy. Many will say, "It's not the daughter's fault she behaves that way," and they are correct. Her parents have done her an incredible disservice. Their desire was to "love" their daughter and bless her, but with what?

As parents we have an awesome responsibility to give our children "all" that they need, not "all" that they want. One of the greatest gifts we can ever give to our children is the gift of character. It is not a gift that causes them to look flashy, rich, or beautiful on the outside. It is a gift that causes them to be beautiful on the inside. But you cannot develop character if you do not master the art of delaying gratification.

Step 10: Use logical consequences rather than punishments.

All effective approaches to discipline emphasize the importance of using logical consequences instead of punishments. What's the difference between the two?

Logical consequences ... are linked in a meaningful way to the child's misbehavior—they "fit" the infraction.

Punishments ... have no meaningful relationship to the misbehavior—they're arbitrary.

Logical consequences ... place a heavy emphasis on allowing the child to repair the problem or make restitution.

Punishments ... place a heavy emphasis on making the child feel bad.

Logical consequences ... when delivered with empathy, force the child to think very hard about his or her poor decisions.

Punishments ... allow the child to project blame for his or her poor choices onto adults.

The Four-Step Consequence Approach

1. Delay the consequence.

   "This is so sad. I'm going to have to do something about this ... but not now. I'll give it some thought and talk to you later."

2. Make a plan with help from others. Before taking action, make sure you have support from others and have plugged all of the potential "holes" in your plan. Typically it is best if the child is the one who solves the problem. Therefore it's often wisest to develop two possible plans:

   a. Some suggestions you can provide the child for making restitution.
   b. A consequence you can deliver just in case the child refuses to solve the problem.

3. Follow the steps for guiding kids to solve their own problems.

   a. Lock in the empathy.

      "What a drag."

   b. Hand the problem back.

      "How are you going to solve this problem?"

   c. Ask permission to share two or three possible solutions.

      "Would you like to hear some ideas?"

   d. Help the child evaluate each solution.

      "How will that work for you?"

   e. Give the "power message."

      "Good luck. Let me know how it works out."

4. Deliver a consequence if the child doesn't solve the problem.

   "How sad, I guess I'll have to take care of this."

Step 11: Expect your child to "repay" you for time and energy you spend listening to his or her defiance, disrespect, or other misbehavior.

> *"Being lied to really drains my energy. How are you planning to put that energy back?"*

Have you ever found yourself trying to think of a logical consequence—just to come up empty-handed? The ***Energy Drain*** approach was created by Foster W. Cline, M.D., to give adults a practical way of creating such consequences. Simply, the child (or teen) is required to replace energy "drained" from the adult by their misbehavior. Let's take a look at the steps:

1. Deliver a strong dose of sincere empathy.

   "This is so sad."

2. Notify the youngster that their misbehavior drained your energy.

   "Oh, Sweetie. When you lie to me [or almost any other misbehavior], it drains energy right out of me."

3. Ask how he or she plans to replace the energy.

   "How are you planning to put the energy back?"

4. If you hear, "I don't know," offer some payback options.

   "Some kids decide to do some of their mom's chores. How would that work? Some kids decide to hire and pay for a baby-sitter—so their parents can go out and relax. How would that work?"

5. If the child completes the chores, thank them and don't lecture.

   "Thanks so much! I really appreciate that."

6. If the child refuses or forgets, don't warn or remind, simply hire someone else to do the job and charge this back to your youngster. ***Remember that actions speak louder than words!***

7. As a last resort, go on strike or sell possessions to pay for the drain.

   "What a bummer. I just don't think I have the energy to take you to Silly Willie's Fun Park this weekend."

   or ...

   "What a bummer. You forgot to do those chores. No problem. I sold your Mutant Death Squad action figure to pay for a baby-sitter tonight. She'll be here at six o'clock."

   Note: Selling a possession that was purchased by the child can create a huge problem. Wise parents prepare for this by buying something special for the child so that the youngster has something that not only is valued, but also was paid for by the parent. This makes it difficult for the kid to say, "Fine! I'll just get some of your stuff and sell it so that I can get mine back!"

   If this were to happen, the parent could simply say, "That's a possibility. If you can find anything in my room that you paid for, I probably won't be able to complain too much. If you take anything that I paid for, don't take it personally if I let the authorities deal with it. That's how I'd handle it with anyone."

9

The E's of Love and Logic

The happiness and unhappiness of the rational, social animal depends not on what he feels but on what he does; just as his virtue and vice consist not in feeling but in doing.

—Marcus Aurelius Antoninus

9

The E's of Love and Logic

Experience is not what happens to a man; it is what a man does with what happens to him.

—Aldous Huxley

In conclusion we will confirm the importance of the three E's of Love and Logic—***Empathy***, ***Example***, and ***Experience***—as well as discuss recommendations that will dramatically improve your ability to communicate effectively with even the most difficult of children. As we have stated previously, children learn through example. Research proves that what we model in our own behavior has powerful influence. Therefore we must be willing to discipline our personal behaviors. Our children also learn through experience. There are natural consequences to our choices, both good and bad. As we have shown in this book, our children learn many of their greatest lessons simply by experiencing natural consequences. As children go through these learning processes, our greatest responsibility as parents, teachers, and counselors is to love and support them with empathy and compassion. We must walk a fine line on which we remain their greatest supporters, encouragers, and fans without stealing from them the consequences they so desperately need in order to grow and learn. How do we do this? We create an environment where our behavior is consistently logical, loving, and empathetic. The Love and Logic strategies shared in this book will aid you in creating a consistent and dependable environment that will nurture children's abilities to succeed in their lives. Love and Logic strategies help children develop into happy, balanced, responsible adults. These strategies work because they focus on finding ways to aid children in meeting their basic needs.

In 1954 Abraham Maslow published his book *Motivation and Personality*, which focused on why some people obtain high levels of success whereas others do not. Maslow was one of the first to teach us that success in tasks involving higher-level thinking requires that certain physical and emotional needs are met first. Simply stated, an individual is very unlikely to realize their full potential unless they are well-fed, feel safe, experience a sense of belonging, feel good about themselves, and so forth. In his book *School Without Failure*, William Glasser furthered this basic line of thought and applied it to the public schools.

Research and real-life classroom experience have shown us that the roots of underachievement and apathy can often lie in unfulfilled basic needs. Children will struggle to learn, grow, and mature in balanced, healthy ways if one or more of the following needs are not met:

1. physical well-being and safety
2. emotional safety
3. respect or love from important adults
4. healthy control over one's day-to-day life
5. a sense of being an important and needed member of a group
6. self-competence of efficacy

When a child is struggling in any area, wisdom would dictate that we consider, *"What basic needs are not being met in this child's life?"* A child cannot focus on other things in their life if they are anxious about their basic needs. Communication plays a critical role in the lives of our children because good communication is the foundation of healthy, connected relationships, and healthy, connected relationships serve as the foundation of our lives.

When examining communication, parents report that they are most frustrated by their teens. Parents tell us that they feel that younger children are easier to talk to. With a little loving encouragement, a younger child can often be coaxed into sharing their feelings. But many parents complain that communicating with their teens is like walking through a mine field. Teenage years bring with them unique challenges. Teenagers are notoriously self-consumed and self-focused, which creates rich soil for the weeds of entitlement to take hold and grow. Therefore our focus in this chapter will be to outline effective strategies to aid parents in developing more effective and connected communication with their teens.

The reality is that teenagers like to talk, usually about themselves. Their worlds are centered on themselves, what they want, when they want it. But teenagers, like all of us, communicate most openly and honestly when they feel safe and have a willing listener. If your communication with them is limited to a halfhearted question, such as "How was your day?" and then you barely listen and answer with an "uh huh" or two, your teen will begin to believe that you are not interested. If the sum total of communication with your teen is "Clean your room!" or "Look at me when I am talking to you!" then your teen will begin to tune you out. In order to keep teens talking, you will need to find a balance between routine chatter, lecturing, and a deeper, more connected conversation. When psychologist Torey Hayden asked several hundred teens what they wished they could talk with their parents about, this was their list:

- ***Family matters:*** Vacations, decisions, rules, curfews, serious illness, money problems.
- ***Controversial issues:*** Sex, lifestyles, drugs.
- ***Emotional issues:*** Parents' feelings about them and other things.
- ***Big whys:*** Why do people go hungry? Why is there war? Other philosophical issues.
- ***The future:*** Work, college, making plans for their life beyond the current home.
- ***Current affairs:*** World and community happenings.
- ***Personal interest:*** Sports, hobbies, friends.
- ***Parents themselves:*** What were parents like at their age? They want to hear stories that show them their parents are real people.[1]

The E's of love and logic—***Experience***, ***Example***, and ***Empathy***—fit perfectly in the context of basic communication. How you choose to

1. Adapted from Karen DeBord, Child Development North Carolina Cooperative Extension, "Parenting Teens," *ERIC Digest.*

communicate with your children at all ages sets the standard for how they should communicate throughout their lives. As you commit to growing and strengthening your connection with your children through powerful, respectful, and effective communication, you are actually teaching them the most important skill necessary for them to develop and maintain successful relationships in every area of their lives.

So how can you improve your communication skills? Learn to listen with appreciation and respect. Great communication is built on great listening. Listening is different than hearing. Hearing is a physiological response to sound. All people who do not suffer physical impairments can hear. But not all those that can hear know how to listen. Listening requires a conscious commitment to learning and understanding. Listening to the thoughts and feelings of another person is a way of showing appreciation and respect. Appreciation and respect, as we have seen, are powerful and effective weapons in the battle against entitlement. It is important not only to listen with appreciation and respect, but also to have many ways of communicating and showing our appreciation and respect to those we care about. Too often we only communicate our negative feelings and reactions to each other. We talk about what we don't like more often than we talk about what we do like in another person or situation. Making time to express our respect and appreciation for others is as critical as listening when it comes to building solid, loving, trusting relationships.

I (Dawn) will share with you a story from my book *Greatness and Children: Learn the Rules* to help me illustrate the importance of this point:

> A teacher in New York decided to honor each of her seniors. She called each student to the front of the class, one at a time. She presented each of them with a blue ribbon imprinted with gold letters which read, "Who I Am Makes a Difference," as she described their unique gifts and talents.
>
> Afterwards the teacher decided to do a class project to investigate what kind of impact recognition and appreciation would have on their community. She gave each of the students three blue ribbons and instructed them to go out and do their own acknowl-

edgment ceremonies, and share the ribbons to keep the appreciation and acknowledgment going.

One of the boys in her class went to a junior executive in a nearby company and gave him a blue ribbon for helping him with his career planning. Afterwards, he gave the man the two extra ribbons, and said, "We're doing a class project on recognition. Would you help me by finding someone to honor to keep this appreciation and acknowledgment going?"

Later that day, the junior executive went to his boss. He told his boss that he admired him for being a creative genius, and presented him with a blue ribbon. The boss seemed surprised. The junior executive then handed his boss the last ribbon and said, "Would you do me a favor? Would you take this extra ribbon and pass it on by honoring someone else? The young boy who first gave me the ribbons is doing a project in school, and they want to keep this recognition ceremony going."

That night the boss came home to his fourteen-year-old son. As they sat down, the father realized that he couldn't remember the last time they had sat down to talk. In fact, these days, the only time they communicated was when they were yelling at each other. The father looked at his son. He was amazed at how quickly time had passed. It seemed like only yesterday he was excited as he watched his son learn to talk and walk; now his son talked back and walked away. The father remembered when he was his son's hero, and how his son used to be so excited when he came home. Their relationship was different now. It was difficult and frustrating to communicate. He loved his son but there never seemed to be a good time to tell him. His son seemed angry and depressed, and his attitude was negative and irritating.

"A very interesting thing happened to me today," the father said. "I was in my office when one of the junior executives came in and told me he admired me. Then he gave me a blue ribbon for being a creative genius. Imagine, me, a creative genius!" the father chuckled as the son smiled. "The ribbon says, 'Who I Am Makes a Difference.' He gave me an extra ribbon and asked me to find someone else to honor. I'm not very good at this sort of thing, as you probably already know, but when I was thinking of who I might give it to, I realized that I wanted to give it to you. My days are really hectic, and when I come home, I don't see much of you. It seems we spend most of our time disconnected. I haven't told you in a long time, but you mean the world to me, son, and you make a real difference in my life. I am happy that you are my son. I don't tell you often enough but I'm proud of you, and I love you!"

His son took the ribbon and held it quietly for a few moments. Without a word, he got up and went to his bedroom. He returned moments later with a brown paper bag and handed it to his father. As the father opened the bag he discovered a loaded gun and a suicide note. "Things have been really hard for me lately, Dad, really hard," the boy confessed.

The father grabbed his son and held him. The boy hugged his dad tightly with one hand, as he held on to the ribbon with the other.

This story is of course a dramatization, but it's a perfect example of the power of communicating appreciation. Human beings need to be noticed. Each of us needs to be recognized. We need to feel that we are loved and understood. We all need to know that who we are makes a difference to someone. When we are willing to express appreciation openly and give it generously, we can transform lives—not only ours, but those of everyone we come in contact with, especially our children.

As the story portrays, appreciation, attention, and recognition are very important; so, what gets yours? If you are anything like many of my clients, your attention is captured by what is wrong, not what is right. It is easy to get sidetracked with thoughts of what we lack. That is how entitlement poisons our relationships and our attitudes.

Here is an important and enlightening exercise. It is one that you might want to try and then teach to your children. Begin by purchasing a journal, one of your choosing—it doesn't matter if it is a notepad, a blank book with lines, or a one-of-a-kind handmade book. Carry it with you for several days. On the first page, describe your life; simply sit down and describe your life. Spend at least fifteen minutes on this assignment, but you can take as much time as you like. When you have completed the description of your life, move on to the second part of the assignment: go for one day, but try to do it without complaining.

Most of my (Dawn's) clients think this exercise is ridiculous because they are sure their complaints are few. (Interestingly, they usually begin the exercise about complaining, with a complaint!) I explain to them that this is an exercise to help them become aware of complaining, even when they don't think they complain. I simply want them to be aware of how many complaints they have within a twenty-four-hour period of time. Then I ask them to keep a journal with them and to jot down how often they catch themselves in the middle of a complaint or negative thought.

So far in my seventeen years of doing therapy, no one has successfully gone twenty-four hours without a complaint. The power in this experiment lies in my clients' realizations that most of the things they complain about, in the big scheme of life, are small and petty. They realize that most of the negative things they whine and complain about with regard to each other are small and petty as well.

Once my clients begin to investigate how often they whine and complain, I ask them to use their journals to write down all of the things for which they are thankful. Most people begin with material or tangible things they are thankful for—their job, their house, their cars, their clothes, their families. As they continue to write, they move toward the more intangible things like love, freedom, friendship, and health. I then ask them to put a monetary value on their freedom, their families, their friendships, their health, their eyes, their legs, and their internal organs. What they discover is that they are rich beyond their wildest imaginations. They begin to recognize how much they have, instead of concentrating on what they perceive they do not have. It works just like the story about my son and his turtles that I shared in Chapter 1.

After they complete their *thank-full* list, I ask my clients to read it three to four times a day over the next few days. Then I ask them to jot down their thoughts and feelings about their lives in their journals and compare them to the first day's journaling. As you can imagine, there is no comparison. Their first description of their lives is filled with complaints, frustration, and lack, the later version filled with gratitude, awareness, and appreciation.

What my clients learn is that appreciation and gratitude are actually good for them. They feel better. They are more hopeful, more optimistic, and more alive. It is a simple concept but extraordinarily powerful. It is something we must remind ourselves of often in order to keep the appreciation alive and the desire to whine and complain at bay.

Appreciation works on many levels simultaneously. It blesses us when we feel it, it blesses us when we share it, and it blesses the world when we teach it. It is a gentle and sincere way to express worth to our children. Being appreciative of others is a wonderful way for children to discover their own sense of worth. Although it costs nothing to live appreciatively, the benefits to all involved are staggering.

An eighteenth-century mother once wrote, "God sends children for another purpose than merely to keep up the race. ... [He sends them] to enlarge our hearts; and to make us unselfish and full of kindly sympathies and affections; to give our souls higher aims; to call out all our faculties to extended enterprise and exertion; and to bring round our firesides bright faces, happy smiles and loving, tender hearts." We believe that appreciation enlarges everyone's heart. If children are to teach us to be unselfish and full of kindly sympathies and affections, to give our souls higher aims, to call out all our talents and energies to use for the benefit of ourselves and others, then we as parents and caregivers of children must return the favor and teach our children to live appreciative, generous, contributing lives as well. The way to ensure that higher aims fill our souls, and that tender affections fill our hearts, is through appreciation. It is pure and simple, and it works.

My (Dawn's) family has a ritual that I believe positively impacts our ability to communicate lovingly with each other. Once every couple of months we gather together in the home for an appreciation ceremony. We take a candle, which we have named the "love candle," and light it. The person holding the candle speaks to all the other people in the room, telling them why he or she appreciates them, and why they are special in his or her life. The love candle is then passed to the next person, who shares his or her feelings of love and appreciation with each person as well. (Some families use a small pillow they have made; others use an object of special importance; one family I know even uses their small dog—the one holding the pet speaks their appreciation to the other members of the family, and then passes on the dog to another member. Pick what fits the personalities in your family.)

It is a wonderful opportunity to speak the appreciative truth that lives in our hearts, but that often isn't spoken. Spoken confirmation of our value inspires us. It creates a win/win environment. It is a gift for the person getting to express his or her appreciation, as well as for the person being appreciated. Communication is exciting, but it does not come naturally; we must learn how to better relate to each other that which is in our hearts. Communication is an area where you can use your creativity. Have a family meeting and brainstorm about ways your family might feel most comfortable showing appreciation. Start a tradition of having a ceremony of your own. We assure you, no one gets tired of hearing that he or she is important.

As I mentioned earlier, not only is listening a critical part of communicating effectively, but it is also a wonderful form of appreciation. It is a form of loving. Even if we can hear at birth, we must learn to listen. The art of listening comprises a set of simple but necessary basic skills. Review the following list to discover how many of these necessary listening skills you have already developed. To describe these skills we will use the acronym:

L.I.S.T.E.N. T.O.

L*ook at the person.* Make eye contact long enough to notice the color of their eyes.

I*nviting posture.* Respect a person's personal space. Express empathy with your body.

S*ense the connection.* Attempt to understand their feelings, mirror appropriate expressions.

T*ake time to reflect.* What are they really saying?

E*xperience their perspective.* Attempt to understand their thoughts, see the world through their lenses.

N*ever attack.* Personal attacks shut communication down!

T*ake a breath.* Don't respond too quickly. Consider what they are saying and consider your response.

O*ffer a respectful response.* Communication is a gift—offer it as one.

Diminishing Teen-Parent Border Disputes with Love and Logic

> *Our goal is to create a beloved community and this will require a qualitative change in our souls as well as a quantitative change in our lives.*
>
> —Martin Luther King, Jr.

For many parents, raising a teenager can feel like living in a war zone. For some, there are daily spats, continuous battles for control, and never-ending frustration. The teenage years are fraught with challenges for both parents and teenagers. While teens fight to understand and define themselves, often thrashing about and lashing out at any perceived control, parents attempt to keep the transformation of their children into adults within some reasonable, safe boundaries. Parents see it as protection, while teens often view it as domination or control. Therefore, the parent-teen war is usually fought over boundaries. There is confusion and disagreement over where the line should be that delineates who controls what area in each other's lives. Each wants complete control. Neither wants to understand, or compromise. Each thinks that they are right and know what is best. Like a border dispute between neighboring countries, these arguments can perpetuate endless no-win battles. Both sides say they want peace, but each wants the other side to make the concessions. Often this is because neither is willing to admit responsibility for their part of the conflict. From the parents' point of view, the sole cause of the strife is their adolescent's complete unreasonableness and total lack of responsibility. And of course the teen sees it in exactly the same way, except in reverse. Both parents and teen feel *entitled* to having their way, which causes them both to feel frustrated and angry.

Let's discuss three major no-win games that teens and parents play that create unproductive, unnecessary, and destructive battles.

I. The "Trivial Pursuit Dispute" Game

Remember the game *Trivial Pursuit*? The object of the game is to focus on trivia. But this focus on trivia in real life can cause unnecessary distress and conflict in our relationships. When I (Dawn) was younger, I asked my mother once how she picked the things that she chose to be really upset about. She said that she asked herself a simple but important question: "Will this matter at Christmas?"

A *Trivial Pursuit* dispute is a dispute that we can find ourselves in the middle of before we have taken the time to ask ourselves if it really matters in the larger scheme of life. Some battles are really important, like drugs, drinking and driving, and unprotected sex, and some are not. If a behavior or choice has the potential to produce a lasting negative effect that will be as important by Christmas as it is now, it is worth fighting about (if the dispute occurs close to Christmas, ask yourself if it will matter by next Christmas). If the situation or event is not worth fighting about, ask yourself, "Why am I choosing to get upset about this issue?"

Many times, discovering the reason behind the reason we are reacting with such passion will bring great insight into our lives. When we take time to explore the motivations behind our reactions, we not only discover important information about ourselves, but also model a self-reflective discipline that aids our children in developing their emotional intelligence.

Each parent has to decide what battles are truly worth fighting. Examples of common battles might include the color of the teen's hair or the cleanliness of their bedroom, the style of clothes they wear, or whether they remember to wear their coats to school when it's cold. A common problem for most parents is their teen's tendency to sleep until noon on the weekends. As a parent you must decide what values and standards you believe are most important and what are the *"give-and-take issues"* that you can actually tolerate.

I (Dawn) will never forget one such opportunity. Corbin, my youngest son, his father, and I were going to a school conference. At this conference we would decide the advanced schedule for my son's junior year. Corbin is a great kid, does very well in school, and is kind and well behaved. None of that seemed to matter to me when he walked out the front door at the end of May (keep in mind that this is in Oklahoma and it is hot in May) with a hooded sweatshirt over another T-shirt, with the hood up and pulled over his wool black beanie, which was pulled down over his ears. To complete the picture, he was wearing a pair of baggy jeans that were ready to fall to his knees, a pair of dark sunglasses, and flip flops, which were making that annoying flapping sound as he walked.

I couldn't believe my eyes. I wondered if he knew that he was going to meet with an adviser to plan his advanced courses for his next school year, or if he thought he was on his way to hold up a convenience store? Everything in me wanted to halt him in his tracks, and make him go back inside to change into something more presentable and less embarrassing for me. I had to hold my lips shut in order to keep myself from making any sarcastic comments about his choice of dress. I closed my eyes for a moment, took a deep breath, and remembering my mother's wisdom, asked myself, "Will this matter at Christmas?" After allowing myself to consider all of the facts about who Corbin was, and what I believed to be most important in his life, the answer for me was no. I took a deep breath and simply relaxed my body and told myself to *"Let it go."* The day turned out to be a wonderful experience. We had a great conference, followed by a lunch filled with wonderful conversation and laughter.

Reflecting back, I realize that, once Corbin got in the car and we started talking, I quickly forgot about what he was wearing. I am happy I had the insight and fortitude to stop and question my immediate reaction to his clothing. There are bigger, more important battles that are worthy of the effort and energy of a fight, but for me, that wasn't one of them. The memory of the day will remain a treasure in my heart. But I really have no doubt that I might have started that day differently: I could have stolen a great experience for both my son and myself by making his choice of clothing the focus of my attention. I am thankful that I stopped to ask myself, "Will the way he is dressed really affect the quality of his conference? Will it really matter, in the larger scheme of life, at Christmas?" I am glad that I made the choice to let it go instead of choosing to play the "*Trivial Pursuit* Dispute" game.

> *The essence of greatness is the ability to choose personal fulfillment in the circumstances where others choose madness.*
>
> —Dr. Wayne W. Dyer

Both Jim and I have spoken to many parents who believe that their adolescents choose certain behaviors solely to make them crazy. Maybe—it's certainly a possibility, but so what? That's not really the point. Some parents fear that if they give in at all, they will lose complete control. Our response is, they never had complete control anyway. From the teen's point of view, the parent is a tyrant, an ogre, and a dinosaur who wants to dominate their every move. And thus the battles continue.

Remember the two basic rules of Love and Logic:

Rule #1: Adults set firm limits in loving ways without anger, lecture, or threats.

Rule #2: When a child causes a problem, the adult hands it back in loving ways.

The Love and Logic philosophy is based on the belief that our children need a sense of control in their lives and that we as parents not only are in charge of allowing them this sense, but also are responsible for enabling it. However, it is up to us as parents to set clear and precise boundaries and parameters. Then we allow the children the freedom to make their choices and provide them with the natural and logical consequences of both their good and their bad choices. It sounds simple and it actually is. But it is not easy. It takes clarity, focus, and most of all, courage.

II. The "Accuse, Misuse, and Abuse" Game (AKA the "Dissing" Game)

You have heard of "Spin the Bottle." It's a kissing game that teenagers often play. The "Dissing" game is different. Instead of kissing each other, in this game you diss each other. This is a game of disrespect. It is a destructive game where we blame, shame, and lower ourselves to calling each other names, which is where the abuse most often comes into play. The goal of a blaming game is to "make the other person wrong," and we usually do not care how disrespectful we have to be, or low below the belt we have to hit, to win the game and accomplish our goal. The object of this game is to label and shame our alleged opponent into admitting that their terrible attitude or lousy behavior is the reason their life isn't functioning according to our standards. This is usually where we blame them for all of their unhappiness, as well as ours. This game is one of the worst we can play with each other. It is destructive because it usually leaves the victims emotionally and sometimes physically wounded. When we accuse, misuse, and abuse each other, we shut down communication completely. There is no way to have a respectful conversation when one or both people are attacking each other. There is never a successful end to these encounters and you should avoid them at all costs. In this game the battles begin with phrases like "You always ..." and "You never ..." or "You are such [a negative] and you will never be [a positive]." As in:

> "You always interrupt me! You never listen to my side of the story."
>
> "You are such a blabbermouth. You will never be able to listen to anyone but yourself."

In order to keep the destructive battles in this game raging, someone must be willing to hit the blaming ball back with a justification like:

> "People wouldn't *have* to interrupt you all the time if you'd ever stop talking! You are an endless spewing fire-hose of negativity and complaints. Besides, you never say anything worth listening to anyway."

We highly recommend that you concentrate on losing as many of these battles as possible. Someone has to have the courage to disengage, and guess what, in most cases it isn't going to be the adolescent. This is where parents must develop great discipline and stop playing the game. Parents must commit to modeling respectful, caring ways to communicate. That is where using Love and Logic techniques can transform your relationship with your teenager. Blaming, shaming, accusing, and calling each other names is never effective, and will never lead to a positive outcome.

III. "The Right Way to Be Wrong" Game

This is a game that people are usually passionate about playing. They play it with each other all the time. It is not a game reserved for teenagers and their parents, even though teens and parents play this game a lot. It doesn't matter what the topic is—politics, the weather, the laws of metaphysics, or the proper way to open an envelope—the point of the verbal standoffs in this game is to prove one point and one point only: that one person is right. This leaves the other person left holding the wrong bag.

At the core of every dispute is the wish to prove that you are someone who knows what you are talking about. This is a game where each of the players wants to command and win respect. The problem is, *commanding* respect is the most ineffective way to get it. This is a game where even when you win, you lose. That all-encompassing desire to be right is often what we use to justify our anger and our rage. And this is a time of rage. Interestingly, you cannot experience rage without first believing that you are *right* about whatever it is that you're raging about. If you examine any situation when you were in a rage, you will discover that you had a story in mind in which you were right and you felt that you were a victim of someone, or something, that was wrong. Rage travels hand in hand with the entitled belief that *being right* is what is important. Some experts purport that this explosion of rage has to do with the increasing pressures of our fast-paced lives. They believe that as life gets faster, we feel more and more hurried, tense, and out of sorts, that there is less time to do anything right, including dealing with emotions. Therefore, this is a game of speed. It is one where we jump to hasty conclusions, burn through our patience, rush to accuse others, and hurry to defend our positions.

By now you understand why this epidemic of rage has gripped our nation. Rage is one of the most frightening and destructive symptoms of entitlement. It is not that this generation is experiencing more pressure than have generations past; instead it is that we believe that we have the right *not* to handle the pressure in mature, responsible, and considerate ways. Rage, like a drug, creates an altered state of consciousness.

> *You become God for a moment,* you
> feel a sense of wounded entitlement,
> *a boundary trespassed, and you*

> *feel wronged. The response is to flare up and set things* right, *redress the injury,* right *the balance, get on top again.*
>
> —Michael Eigen

Michael Eigen, a psychologist and an associate clinical professor at New York University,[2] believes that rage has become a social addiction, and sadly, our adolescents are one of the populations that are extremely vulnerable to developing this social addiction. What if all addictions are really simply symptoms of entitlement? What if addictions are really habits created out of entitled beliefs that each person has a right to abuse drugs, alcohol, people, and him- or herself? Many will argue that alcoholism is a disease; if so, I believe that entitlement is the virus that carries it. I also believe that rage is simply a very bad habit. It is something that we have grown accustomed to using instead of developing higher-level communication skills. Eigen tells us:

> If I had to pinpoint a single element to start with (that causes this outburst called rage) ***it is the sense of being right.*** Look at and keep looking at, the feeling of being right, and whether this feeling gives you the right to hurt others, or to exercise power over them, subtly or overtly. I believe the human race needs to sit with this sense of being right, turn it this way and that, see how it works, go beyond it in the family, in the workplace—and between nations.[3]

The desire to be right, and to *right* things in our direction, is one of entitlement's greatest covert weapons. The insidious certainty that comes with feeling right invites entitlement to invade our most sacred spaces. As human beings, we would rather be right than just about anything

2. Michael Eigen, author of *Rage* (Wesleyan University Press, 2002), *Ecstasy* (Continuum International, 2001), and *Psychic Deadness* (Jason Aronson, 1996). Emphasis added.
3. Ibid.

else. We will sacrifice love, connection, friendship, happiness—whatever it takes for the opportunity to be right. Why? Simply because we desperately want to win this game. We forget that our perspective is colored by the lenses through which we view life. We forget that other people's perspectives may not be the same as ours, and that this does not necessarily make them wrong.

The danger of playing this game occurs when we fall in love with our story about being right. While playing this game, we develop deep attachments to our beliefs about what is right. We don't usually care if being right keeps us from feeling the happiness we long for, or if being right keeps us from success at work. Entitlement tells us that the only important thing is winning, but winning this game actually steals what is valuable to our lives and relationships, and leaves us rigidly and righteously holding the trophy that proves we are right about being victims of our perceived injustices.

I (Dawn) went to a parenting seminar over two decades ago. I had just given birth to my first son, Tony, and the love I felt for him was ineffable. I was very angry with my parents for decisions they had made while raising me. My goal for attending this seminar was to learn to be a better parent than I perceived my parents to be.

The morning portion of the workshop shocked and surprised me. I had gone there to learn to be a successful parent. Instead, I found myself in a room full of adults telling stories about how their parents had failed them. Not that I minded. I was just waiting to get up the courage to stand and share my sad horror story of alcoholism, drugs, poverty, irresponsibility, and unstable everything. People had great sympathy for these stories of abuse and neglect, and I certainly believed a little sympathy should be coming my way.

One woman stood up and told everyone that she had been married four times. She confessed that she had gone to a therapist who had helped her trace her difficulty back to her childhood. She began to tell the sad story of her trauma. She explained that she was one of four children. One day when she was five, her mother had a big dinner planned at their home for her father's boss. She said that the children were excited because the mother announced that she had to have the day to cook and clean, and asked the children if they would rather spend the day at the movies, or go to the local park and swim. They excitedly selected swimming. The mother then announced that they could each invite a friend, since it was going to be a several-hour affair. She put the children in the van, picked up their four friends, and dropped them all off at the pool. It was secure, and there were many lifeguards, so many parents dropped their children off to swim while they ran boring errands that the children would hate.

The woman remembered the day vividly. She recounted it in detail. She explained that the day had been great fun, but that when her mother came to collect the eight children, she realized that she had forgotten her towel. Without telling her mother, she ran back to the edge of the pool to collect it. When she arrived back to where the van had been parked, it was gone. In all of the confusion, and hurry of the day, the mother had not taken a head count and did not realize that she had forgotten her little girl until they arrived home. The mother was panicked. She left her chicken to burn, her table unset, and rushed back to find her little girl sobbing. Everyone was miserable. The dinner was ruined, and so was the little girl's life.

She determined that her mother forgot her because she didn't love her. She said she had come to realize that her four failed marriages were her mother's fault. Because her mother forgot her that day, the little girl decided that no one would love her. Everyone would leave her sooner or later, and guess what, she was right.

She wore the four failed marriages like a badge of courage on her sleeve. She used them as conclusive evidence that she had no value and could not succeed, or ever be secure in a relationship. She was righteous, poised in her certainty, and unwavering in her story.

The instructor listened intently and then asked the woman, "How many times did your mother remember you?"

"What do you mean?" stuttered the woman.

"I mean, how many times did your mother remember you?"

"I don't understand the question," the woman said, shifting her weight from one leg to the other. "I just told you *she forgot me.*"

"Yes, you did. Now I would like you to tell me how many times she remembered you."

"You mean every day when I was growing up?" the woman asked as her face began to flush.

"Yes, you have shared an experience from one day of your life; now share with us some of the rest."

"Well, my mother didn't forget me any of the others," defended the woman.

"Okay, so how many times did she remember you? Did she take you to school and pick you up?"

"Yes."

"Every school day?"

"Yes."

"Did she take you other places as well?"

"Yes."

"Did she do this every day?"

"Well, almost every day," said the woman, looking confused.

"How many times would you say she remembered you?"

"Throughout my whole life?"

"Yes. Would it be one hundred?"

"No, many more than that."

"How many would you guess?"

"Thousands probably."

"Thousands?"

"Yes."

"And she forgot you once?"

"But ... it was her job to remember me. Parents are supposed to remember their children." The woman was on the verge of tears.

"And I thought she did, in fact, thousands of times. Is that correct?" the instructor asked.

"I guess so," the woman answered hesitantly.

"So although your mother remembered you thousands of times, you picked the one time she forgot you to base your life and value on? Do you know why?"

"I wanted to make her pay for forgetting me. I wanted her to see that forgetting a child can negatively affect their whole life. And *I was right*, it has."

"Maybe, but what if you have sacrificed feeling loved and safe, having successful committed relationships, friendships, a powerful relationship with your mom, and many other blessings, so that you could be right? Has being right been worth what it has cost you?"

"Yes ... I mean no ... I don't know anymore." The woman began to cry.

"Very good," the instructor said. "You have taken your first step away from the limitations forced upon you by the certainty of being right."

When we are not sure, we are alive.

—Graham Greene

How to Stop Playing War Games with Teens

Many parents come to Jim and me for answers on how to stop playing war games with their teenagers. There are no simple prescriptions to make parent-teen relations tension-free. Adolescence is a time of individuation, and some tension is natural and to some extent even necessary, but there are some general principles that can help to greatly reduce the frequency and intensity of these battles. First, and most important, remember to approach situations with family members, as well as those you care about, with respect, appreciation, genuine empathy, and Love and Logic. Use opportunities to teach your children through experience, example, and empathy.

- ***Pick your priorities.*** To avoid getting caught in the "Trivial Pursuit Dispute" game, focus on your minimal requirements for your teen. By minimal requirements, we don't mean your *Wish List* (get straight A's, speak several languages, keep their room spotless, always speak politely), but rather what he or she *needs* to do to stay in your good graces (go to school and get passing grades, keep their room clean enough that it's appropriate for more than insects to live in, contribute to the family's betterment). Focusing on minimal requirements doesn't mean that you stop expecting that your teen will grow up into a happy, well-adjusted, responsible adult. But it does mean carefully and thoughtfully picking your battles and making compromises whenever possible. Remember to ask yourself, "Will this really matter at Christmas?"

- ***Life is a gift—keep the present.*** Life may be a game, but more importantly, life is a gift. Each breath, each relationship, each experience, whether good or bad, is a gift, but we have to choose to view them that way. It is up to us to stop playing destructive, unproductive games and instead treasure the gift that each experience can be for us. We must not forget to live life as a present, as well as live life in the present. It is only when we forgive the past and look toward the future that we are free to cherish the value of the moment. Today is all we really have. Whether we choose to live life as a game or not, the present is all that really exists. To avoid falling into the blame and shame games, focus on what you want to happen, not on what's gone wrong or whose fault it was. In order to continue to blame and accuse we must continue to bring up past episodes. When we focus on making the other person wrong, we have a tendency to accumulate data to prove our point. This way we can use months' or years' worth of examples in every accusation. For example, instead of saying, "You never listen to me," try "I will be happy to communicate my feelings about this situation when I feel that you would like to listen." Can you see the difference? One relies on an accumulation of past experiences, while the second communicates needs, effectively and respectfully, in the present. Instead of saying, "You're such a slob," try "I reward cleanliness with my time and attention."
- ***Own the color of your lenses—feelings aren't facts.*** Instead of battling about who's right and who's wrong, admit from the start that you are seeing things from your own point of view. Consider that everyone views the world through different lenses. Consider the different per-

spectives that would result if you saw the world through yellow lenses and someone else saw the world through blue lenses. What you might see as yellow, that other person could just as legitimately claim to be blue. Understand that your lenses are most likely a different color than the lenses your teen is wearing. As Stephen Covey tells us in his book *The Seven Habits of Highly Successful People,* "Seek first to understand, and then to be understood." Have conversations that will enable you to understand each other's perspectives. Rather than wrangle over what you consider to be objective facts ("It's true, you *do* sneer at everything I say"), cut right to the subjective reality ("It *seems to me* that you sneer at me a lot—at least that's how it feels"). By doing this, you make the discussion about your feelings—which is really the more important point, isn't it? Remember that insisting on being right can make everything important in your relationship feel wrong.

- ***Fight for your children, not with them.*** If you make an effort to remain respectful, use your empathetic response, listen without interrupting, and refrain from shaming, accusing, or calling your teen names, chances are that sooner or later your teen will follow your lead and do the same, especially if that is the only game in town. Kids want to play with you; they simply need more productive games, with better-defined rules. Choose to model appropriate behavior that you want your children to emulate.

Don't misunderstand us, parents need to be willing to fight, but the fight needs to be for your children, not with them. This is a critical distinction. When teenagers do things that are clearly dangerous, such as getting involved in drugs, unprotected sex, or criminal activities, they need parents who will take on their behaviors forcefully. They need parents who will insist that harmful behaviors stop immediately. But don't waste your energy on trivial battles that do not serve you or your children. Don't play games that no one can win. By focusing on what is really important in your children's lives, you'll discover that you have more strength to deal with important problems that can arise, and that the games you play with your kids will be moments of fun and enjoyment instead of fiascoes.

Afterword

The purpose of this book has been to examine how entitlement can steal your success, your happiness, and your dreams. Our hope is that you have begun to understand the concept of entitlement and its powerful impact on your life and the lives of your children, and that you will commit to fighting against the wrath of entitlement with every resource you can. Living lives filled with Love and Logic can serve to protect you against the wrath of entitlement and actually add success and happiness back into the equation. Throughout this book, we have provided you with the tools you need to aid your children in becoming the great people they were meant to be, and we hope that the information has been clear, practical, and life-changing. For many of you it has given voice to what you already believe, as well as provided the courage to continue what you are doing in the face of much of the misinformation and confusion running rampant in our society. Entitlement and its cancerous tentacles have infected every area of our lives. But the cure for the wrath of entitlement is simple. The answer lies in filling minds with simple but effective strategies of logic and filling our judgmental and controlling hearts with love.

A day dawns, quite like other days;
but in that day and in that hour the
chance of a lifetime faces us.

—Maltbie Babcock

Other Materials by Jim Fay

Jim Fay has published over three hundred books, audios, videos, and articles, including:

Avoiding Power Struggles with Kids

Developing Character in Teens

Didn't I Tell You to Take Out the Trash?!

Four Steps to Responsibility

Grandparenting with Love and Logic

Helicopters, Drill Sergeants, and Consultants

Hope for Underachieving Kids

Hormones and Wheels

Love and Logic Magic for Early Childhood

Love and Logic Magic When Kids Drain Your Energy

Love and Logic Magic When Kids Leave You Speechless

Love and Logic Solutions

Love Me Enough to Set Some Limits

Parenting Teens with Love and Logic

Parenting with Love and Logic

Put the Fun Back Into Parenting

Raising the Odds for Responsible Behavior

Shaping Self-Concept

Teaching with Love and Logic

Trouble-Free Teens

... and other products too numerous to list.

For information on the many products authored by Jim Fay, call 800-338-4065 to receive a free catalog, or visit www.loveandlogic.com.

About the Authors

Jim Fay

The legendary Jim Fay began his career as a teacher and for over three decades served in public, private, and parochial schools. He spent seventeen years as a school principal and administrator, and for nearly thirty years has been a public speaker. Jim has served as a national and international educational consultant to schools, parent organizations, counselors, mental health organizations, and the U.S. military.

Jim believes his major accomplishment in life is the development of a unique philosophy of practical techniques for enhancing communication between children and adults, known as Love and Logic. Jim has taken complex problems and broken them down into simple, easy-to-use concepts and techniques that can be understood and used by anyone. Hundreds of thousands of people have expressed how Love and Logic has enhanced their relationships with their children.

Jim is one of America's most sought after presenters in the area of parenting and school discipline. His practical techniques are revolutionizing the way parents and professionals deal with children, to help them become responsible, thinking people and enhance their own self-concept.

Other Materials by Dawn Billings

Books by Dawn Billings include:

The ABC's of Becoming Great

The ABC's of Great Networking

The ABC's of Great People Skills

The ABC's of Great Relationships (workbook)

Choose to Be Great (e-workbook)

Entitled to Fail, Endowed to Succeed: America's Journey Back to Greatness

52 Ways to Heal a Relationship

Greatness and Children: Learn the Rules

Greatness Is Never An Accident

Inspiring Quotes and Poems of Greatness

It Started Out So Good

The Perfect Heart

Possibilities: Awakening the Leadership Potential Within (featuring *The ABC's of Great Leadership*)

Possibilities II: Stories from the Heart That Feed the Mind

The Top 50 Low Cost and No Cost Retention Strategies (coauthored with Dawn's son Corbin)

What Went Wrong with Our Relationship

About the Authors

Dawn Billings

Dawn Billings, M.A., is a licensed professional counselor (LPC) specializing in greatness and leadership for over a decade. Dawn magically weaves historical and statistical information with stories that touch lives in ways that can change the direction of hearts and create a better world, while giving down-to-earth recommendations for solving difficult problems.

Dawn believes that her most defining role is that of mother. She has two sons, to which her books and her life are dedicated. Tony is twenty-five and Corbin is sixteen. Dawn is founder and president of To Touch A Life, a Tulsa-based company dedicated to promoting her professional and personal philosophy. Dawn is a highly sought after speaker and trainer who specializes in the entitlement issues that are currently plaguing our society, starting with our children and ending with our highest-paid leaders. Dawn teaches powerful, effective communication, conflict resolution, and the importance of integrity. Dawn has been in private practice for fifteen years, working with individuals, couples, and what she loves most, families.

Index